THE TILT, COBHAM.

Sep 4th 1920

Miss Combe

To T. TIDY,

Practical Chimney Sweep, Window Cleaner, &c.

	£ s. d.
June 1st Sweeping Kitchen Chimney & Cleaning Flues also Copper Flues to Lodge	6 0
" 9th Sweeping 1 Bedroom, Drawing & Dining Room Chimneys	13 6
14th & 15th Sweeping Pantry Chimney to Hot Water Boiler & Flues also Smoke room & Housemaids Sitting room Sweeping Chimney & Cleaning Flues To Boiler & Furnace which last home & Conservatory	2 2 6
" 20th Sweeping Kitchen Chimney & Cleaning Flues	
Carried Forward	

49, ALBERT EMBANKMENT,
VAUXHALL, S.E.

AND AT

HIGH STREET,
COBHAM, SURREY,

30 Sept 1919

C. H. Combe Esq

W. BROWN,

Saddler & Harness Manufacturer.

All Orders punctually attended to and executed. Contracts taken.

		£ s. d.
	...les @ 3/6	7
	@ 3/6	7 6
5 Sept Tub soft soap		1 10 6
23 " 25 Yards Waggon rope		14 9
	£3 - 6 - 9	

Paid Oct 1/19

W M Brown

With Thanks

H. C. Combes Esq

Bought of W. H. SMITH & SON,

Booksellers and Newsagents,

.... COBHAM. .... Railway Station

At which please pay this Account.

N.B.—It is requested that the Remittance be accompanied by this Bill.
R 9 100,000 4 20

	£ s. d.
Col: Repingtons Memoirs 2 Vols	2 2 -

RECEIVED
WITH THANKS
30 OCT 1920
p.p. W. H. SMITH & SON.
T. C. Mogg

BOUGHT OF

R. F. LUCAS, BOOT MAKER, HIGH STREET, COBHAM.

M C H Coombe Esq :: *Nov: 3rd 1919*

'K' SHOES

are consummate in style, in form, and in craftsmanship.

Every 'K' carries the prestige of a Half-century's Renown.

	£ s. d.
Suit to measure supplied to Arthur Adams	5 5 0

R Lucas

With Thanks

AN ESTATE FOR ALL SEASONS

A History of Cobham Park, Surrey
and its Owners and Occupiers

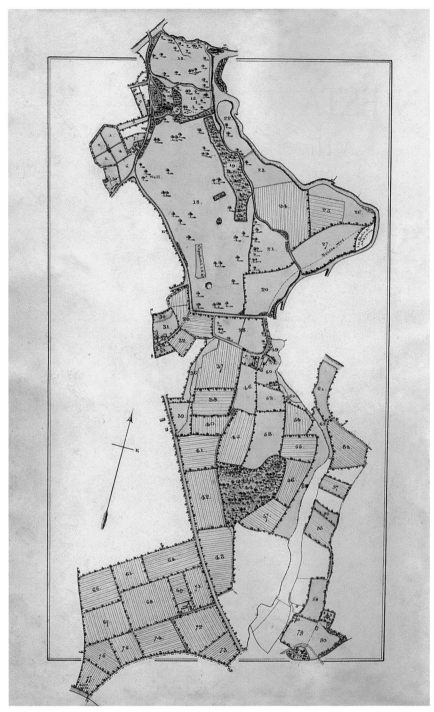

Cobham Park in 1822. From Thomas Crawter's Estate Terrier. This plan shows the
extent of the estate in the time of Harvey Combe junior, 'Young Harvey'. The estate
stretches from Downside Bridge in the north to the parish boundary in the south.

AN ESTATE FOR ALL SEASONS

A History of Cobham Park, Surrey
and its Owners and Occupiers

David Taylor

Strutt & Parker, managing agents of the Cobham Park estate for nearly
one hundred years, are pleased to have been involved in the production of
this book which celebrates the Combe family's bicentenary at Cobham.

Phillimore

2006

Published by
PHILLIMORE & CO. LTD
Shopwyke Manor Barn, Chichester, West Sussex, England
www.phillimore.co.uk

ISBN   1-86077-431-8
ISBN 13   978-1-86077-431-7

Printed and bound in Great Britain by
THE CROMWELL PRESS
Trowbridge, Wiltshire

CONTENTS

LIST OF ILLUSTRATIONS

Frontispiece: Thomas Crawter's plan of Cobham Park in 1822

Between pages 20/21

Illustration Acknowledgements

Permission for the use of the following illustrations is gratefully acknowledged: Bonhams, 28; The British Library, 9, 10, 43; The British Museum, 24; Dominic Combe, frontispiece, 18, 20, 33, 34, 36, 37, 44, 47-52, 54, 55, 57, 58, 60-80, 82-89, 92-109, 111-142; Guildhall Art Gallery, City of London, 39; Guildhall Library, City of London, 40, 41, 42; House of Lords Records Office, 6; Huntington Library, San Marino, California, 21, 22; Norman & Beryl Kitz, 31; National Gallery of Ireland, 11; National Portrait Gallery, 15, 26, 27; New York Genealogical & Biographical Society, 53; Surrey History Centre, 38; Surrey History Service, 12, 19, 56; V&A Picture Library, 25.

    Author's collection: 3, 4, 5, 35, 45, 46, 59, 66, 90, 91 and 110.

INTRODUCTION

Flowers in the garden, meat in the hall,
A bin of wine, a spice of wit,
A house with lawns enclosing it,
A living river by the door,
A nightingale in the sycamore!

These lines by Robert Louis Stevenson could well have been written of Cobham
Park with its lawn which sweeps down to the lake beyond which is the river Mole
– the 'living river'. There are nightingales on nearby Bookham Common, so who
is to say that they cannot be found in Cobham Park!

In 1981 Logica, who then rented Cobham Park mansion for use as offices, asked
me to write an account of the history of the building. I was very much aware that the
small booklet which I eventually produced hardly did justice to the subject, especially
as there was still so much of the earlier history that remained unknown. In 2004 I was
invited by Dominic Combe to undertake the sorting and cataloguing of the very large
and important collection of deeds and other papers that existed. These related both
to the estate and to his family, who came to Cobham in 1806. What was originally
planned as a six-month job is only now nearing completion and there is still work
to be done. My job as estate archivist has provided me with a unique opportunity
to try to understand how the estate developed. This has been both frustrating and
challenging. However, on the whole, it has been a very rewarding task, especially as
the early history of the site emerged from the mists of the Middle Ages.

One thing that soon emerged was that earlier assumptions that the former
Downe Place had stood on the site of the present Cobham Park were incorrect. An
archaeological excavation undertaken in 2005 now seems to locate the ancient seat
of the Downe family as having stood on the site of the present Down Farm – now
the Home Farm of the Cobham Park Estate. In peeling back the layers, widening
the search for information beyond local sources, it has become clear that the house
that stood on the site of the present Cobham Park mansion from about 1730 to 1870
was probably designed by the noted architect Roger Morris. Whilst the destruction
of that house is much to be regretted, the present house represents a tour de force
of the highpoint of the architecture of the Victorian age with all its confidence,
splendour and technical innovation.

Whilst working as estate archivist I was successful in obtaining a Master's degree in Historical Research. My dissertation focused on the lives of three generations of the Combe family in the 19th century who transformed themselves from brewers to country squires. During this work it became evident that there was now enough material to write a more definitive history of Cobham Park and its owners and occupiers. The result is this book which, combined with *Cobham – A History* and my other local history publications, should help provide a better understanding of the development of this part of Cobham.

In acknowledging thanks, Dominic Combe must be at the top of the list as, without his enthusiasm and support, none of this would have been possible. The firm of Strutt & Parker, which manages the estate, has also made a valuable contribution and I am particularly grateful to Kate Moisson and Mark Juniper. Peter Edwards, Elizabeth Einberg, Judie English, George Howard, Steven Parissien, John Pile, Julian Pooley, David Robinson and Dennis Turner, all experts in their own fields, have allowed me to pester them from time to time with my many questions. My thanks also to the staff at the Surrey History Centre – a unique repository of the county's documented history.

Cobham Park and its estate remains a rare survivor in a part of England constantly under pressure from the threat of development. Its survival is largely due to the Combe family and I therefore offer this book as a tribute to mark the two hundredth anniversary of their arrival in Cobham in 1806.

DAVID TAYLOR

1

EARLY DAYS

Against the timeline of history, Cobham Park is a fairly new creation. It was not until the early part of the 18th century that the first 'big house' was built here and attempts were made to create around it a suitable parkland setting from what had been a largely medieval agricultural landscape. However, the history of the site and the surrounding area is much older and people have lived in these parts since early times.

Cobham Park lies just to the south of the centre of modern Cobham and stretches from the river Mole in the north to the hamlet of Downside in the south. The road to Horsley marks its western boundary and the eastern boundary follows the course of the river Mole between Downside Mill and Cobham centre. The present house, built in 1872, is at least the third house to occupy this site and has recently been converted into luxury apartments with other new accommodation close by. Although what was once home to one family is now home to many, the park and the surrounding estate remain in the hands of the family who first made their home here two hundred years ago. It is thanks to that family and their careful management and stewardship of this land that this part of Cobham has remained largely unspoilt despite economic and other pressures. During their time at Cobham Park this family created not only a home for themselves but also a centre for the local community. Many local families found work on the estate – often for two or more generations. The family who owned the estate took their responsibilities seriously and in the days before the welfare state it was they who helped to provide Cobham with many of its public services and amenities including a school, a fire engine, a hospital and a village hall. They also had a say in the running of local affairs and were involved in the coming of the railway. The spiritual life of the parish was another of their concerns and they had the right to appoint Cobham's vicars. The Combe family were involved in all these activities and much more and it is their story, together with that of their predecessors at Cobham, that will be told in the following chapters.

When the Combe family came here in 1806 they opened a new chapter in the history of Cobham Park by purchasing a number of neighbouring properties which became the Cobham Park Estate. And so in the following chapters it is necessary to consider not just the house and its park but the whole estate and the history of that area as a microcosm of the history of Cobham.

Cobham Park is an area of lowland, parts of which are subject to the regular flooding by the river Mole. The park is crossed by a small watercourse that runs from a point just to the east of the house to the river Mole close to Downside Mill. A little further downstream from this point another channel runs east to west across the large bend of river, creating what is virtually an island opposite Cobham Mill. In some early records this is referred to as the 'the old river'. Quite why it is described in this way is a puzzle. As far as is known the river Mole has always followed its present course to the south of the Tilt and round by Cobham Mill. It is possible that this watercourse may have been used to manage the flow of water and help control drainage of adjoining land. The highest land within the park is the down, or dune, a high 'whale-backed' feature which rises steeply from the western bank of the river opposite the Tilt to a height of about 125 feet above sea level. The geological map for this area shows an area of Bagshot Beds capped by gravel on the level summit of this feature. This is the down which gave its name both to the family who lived here in early times and to their home of Downe Hall, or Downe Place, and ultimately to the settlement of Downside that developed close by.

A Deodatus de Dunes is known to have had land in Cobham in the reign of King John. The records of Chertsey Abbey, who then owned the manor of Cobham, state that in the time of Abbot Medmenham (1261-72) Henry de Doune conveyed two Bookham bondsmen to the abbot in exchange for the abbot's bondsman, Ralph Blunt of Bookham and his family and all his chattels.[1] A William de la Dune held the royal office of Keeper of the Hanaper[2] and state documents of Edward I dated at Cobham strongly suggest royal visits to Downe Hall between 1292 and 1306.[3] For many years it was thought that Downe Hall or Downe Place, home of the Doune family, had stood on the site of Cobham Park mansion. Recent research now points to it as having been on the site of Down Farm where excavation has produced evidence of life from the late Saxon period.[4] But even before then it is likely that prehistoric people made their homes on the down.[5] This area of highland would have made an excellent site on which to live. There was a good supply of water nearby and timber was prolific. The high ground provided safety in time of flood and perhaps even in time of attack from unfriendly neighbours. Admittedly the archaeological evidence for this is sparse. A clay loom weight was found on the down some years ago[6] and flint tools and scrapers were also found when the route of the M25 motorway was cut through neighbouring Muggeridge Wood and Down Wood.[7] The landscape would have been an ideal occupational site from the earliest days.[8]

Cobham is an ancient place. There was a settlement on Leigh Hill to the north-east of the village at the time of the Iron Age.[9] The remains of a Roman bathhouse were excavated at Chatley Farm, south of the parish, in the middle of the last century.[10] Domesday Book (1086) records the manor of Cobham as then being owned by the Abbot and monks of St Peter's Abbey at Chertsey and Cobham is likely to have been one of the estates given to the Abbey at its foundation in A.D. 673 by Frithuwold, Viceroy of Surrey. At the time of this grant Cobham was known as Getinges which means the 'people or followers of Get'.[11] It is not known whether Getinges simply referred to Cobham or whether it included lands in other parts of Surrey. Cobham later became Cove(n)ham which either refers to its position in the bend, or cove, of the river, or is derived from a personal name and may have once been Cofa's Ham. Current research by the author and others suggests that modern-day Cobham was originally an area of dispersed settlement with small farms scattered around the parish.

Henry I granted a right of Free Warren to the Abbots of Chertsey to hunt with dogs in their Surrey properties, and to take foxes, hares, pheasants and wild cats. They could also enclose when they wished a park at Cobham for hunting and could take therein anything they liked.[12] It has been suggested that this was the Morelspark referred to in later manorial surveys and which lay in the Downside area. At the time of this grant Cobham, like most of Surrey, was within Windsor Forest, and it was profitable for the king to grant landowners the privilege of destroying animals harmful to the beasts of the royal chase. It was not until 1190 that the knights of Surrey offered Richard I 200 marks that 'they might be quit of all things that belong to the forest from the water of the Wey to Kent and from the street of Guildford as far as Surrey stretches'.[13] After this time Windsor Forest came no closer to Cobham than Byfleet Bridge.

Although the manor of Cobham was the largest within the ancient parish, it was but one of a number of manors and 'reputed manors'. Downside is sometimes referred to as 'a reputed manor'. This may indicate that it was created out of the original Chertsey holding – perhaps by William de la Dune to match his standing as a royal officer. The manor of Cobham was managed from Cobham Court, which was the home of the Abbey's bailiff. It was here in the medieval period that the Courts Baron and Leet were held, dealing with property transactions and minor misdemeanours. Cobham Court stands not far from the parish church of St Andrew which dates from the middle of the 12th century. It seems likely that Chertsey Abbey, in an attempt to better manage their estate at Cobham and presumably increase revenues for the Abbey church, attempted to achieve some measure of nucleation by laying out Church Street with regular building plots. Additionally a charter was obtained from King Stephen for holding a market, possibly at Street Cobham on the important road which led from London to Southampton and the west of England.

It is not known how the people of Cobham fared during the Black Death in the 14th century. However, the fact that the Bishop of Winchester held an ordination in Cobham for a large number of priests from around the south of England when the Black Death was at its peak seems to suggest that Cobham avoided the worst excesses of the plague, which carried off about a third of this country's population. As the country recovered from the Black Death and the famine which had preceded it, so it moved into a more settled period. At this time the lands now forming Cobham Park and its estate were owned by the Abbot and monks of Chertsey Abbey and, in the 15th century, we have the first written records relating to this part of Cobham.

CITIZEN AND FISHMONGER
OF LONDON

On 8 December in the seventh year of the reign of Edward IV (1468) the Abbot of Chertsey granted to Robert Bardsey of Kingston upon Thames 'a certain several croft called Groverscrofte and one several close ... called briggeland and certain underwritten lands and meadows ... lying in the fields called Dounefelde, Westcrofte and Chirchfeld and elsewhere in Cobham.' The grant was made in consideration of 'the faithful services and counsels paid to them before these times' by Bardsey and 'with the unanimous assent of the whole Chapter of the monastery'.[1] This is the earliest known documentary reference that can positively be identified with what is now Cobham Park.

On 4 April 1468 the Bishop of Winchester ratified to Robert Bardsey 'citizen and fishmonger of London' a lease of Bishop's Hall, Kingston.[2] This property lay between what is now Thames Street and the river.[3] Bardsey was a prominent member of the Kingston community and a trustee of the Kingston Bridge Endowment.[4] He was probably present in the town on 1 October 1467 when Edward IV came there with most of the leading nobles of the land to hold a council to agree the terms of his sister Margaret's marriage to Charles, Duke of Burgundy.

Quite what 'faithful services and counsels' Bardsey had performed for Chertsey Abbey is not known. Perhaps he supplied the monks with their all-important diet of fish. The fact that Bardsey was a devoted churchman is confirmed by letters patent granted to him by Edward IV on 14 May 1477 for the foundation of a religious fraternity of the Holy Trinity in the parish church of All Saints, Kingston upon Thames.[5] The fraternity was to consist of two wardens and of clerks or laymen, both men and women. Bardsey granted an annuity of £6 13s.4d. to maintain a priest to sing mass in the Trinity Chapel at Kingston. At least part of the income from the Cobham lands was to help maintain the Kingston fraternity.[6]

Robert Bardsey's wife was Agnes, the daughter of William Skerne, a prosperous Kingston merchant.[7] In 1459 Skerne had been granted licence to found a chantry in honour of the Blessed Virgin and the Holy Body of Christ in All Saints.[8] Bardsey was one of the feoffees, or trustees, of the property given for the endowment of this chantry.[9]

It is tempting to link Bardsey's holding at Groverscrofte in Cobham with Roberto ate Grove who was taxed 13d. in 1332.[10] Dounefeld, Westcrofte and Chirchfield, also named in the grant to Bardsey, were three of the old open fields of Cobham.[11]

Dounefeld lay to the south of the present Cobham Park mansion; Westcrofte was on the opposite site of the road leading from Cobham to Horsley, and Chirchefeld, the largest, lay between Church Street and the old Portsmouth Road. It was the existence of this last field that kept the communities of Church Cobham and Street Cobham apart.

Groverscrofte contained one acre and lay 'between the said close called Briggeland' on the northern part and 'between the said field [Dounefeld] on the southern part and 'the common King's way there' on the western part. A croft is usually interpreted as a garden, or paddock, depending on its size.[12] From this description it can be deduced that Groverscrofte was approximately in the area now occupied by Cobham Park mansion and Briggeland was slightly to the north and was, as its name suggests, close to Downside Bridge which was known at this time as Little Bridge to distinguish it from the Great Bridge, or Cobham Bridge, at the foot of Painshill. In early times the river had been crossed by a ford but it is likely that a bridge was constructed here at an early date because of the importance of the crossing. In order to reach another of their manors at Great Bookham, the monks of Chertsey Abbey would have travelled from Chertsey to Cobham and, after crossing the river, followed the old road which then lay across Bookham Common and on to Dorking. In 1324 this is referred to as 'the king's highway' and, in 1406, it was 'the Royal Way which leads from Coueham [Cobham] towards Pollesden'. This road originally followed a course to the east of its present route through what is now Cobham Park and was probably moved to its present position when the park was enlarged in the 18th century.[13]

The grant to Bardsey lists all the other lands which formed part of Groverscrofte and which were scattered in Dounefelde, Westcrofte and Chirchfelde. In Dounefelde, to the south of Groverscrofte, there were five acres called Broksere which probably took its name from Roger and Margaret Broke who conveyed land to Bardsey in 1478.[14] Broksere lay to the east of 'le Gravelpit in Dounefelde' which adjoined the road to Horsley and which was probably used for extracting gravel for roads and building purposes. Other lands named in the grant to Bardsey include 'one acre called Skirwittes in Dounefelde', a rood of land 'in a place called 'Austy', three roods of land in Dounefelde 'upon Balleshelde between the common way on the western part and the land pertaining to the tenement of Douneplace on the northern part'. 'Thorncroft' lay next to 'Mersfield', and there were three roods of land in 'Waterlande in a certain place called Brodemede Forde'. It is difficult to pinpoint with any accuracy exactly where all these lands were. However, what emerges is a patchwork of small holdings scattered in Dounefelde and which appear, by this date, to have been already enclosed.

In addition to their lands in Kingston and Cobham the Bardseys also held property in Ewhurst, Wotton and Ockley.[15] It is unlikely that the Bardseys farmed the Cobham land themselves; they were almost certainly sub-leasing. In the 14th century 'Edmund, son and heir of Robert Bardsey' was involved in litigation concerning land at Cobham and elsewhere. From 1500 to 1515 'Peter, son of Robert Bardsey' was involved in an action with 'Richard Clerk and Aubrey, his wife' concerning the detention of deeds relating to the manor of Loakes in Chipping Wycombe, Buckingham.[16] Aubrey was Edmund Bardsey's widow and Richard Clerk was Aubrey's second husband. A piece of land in what is now called Plough Meadows was later described as 'once Clerk's'. The relationship of Robert, Peter and Edmund is confusing. Another deed describes Peter, 'citizen and fishmonger of London' as the 'son and heir of Edmund Bardsey'.[17] In 1522 Peter Bardsey conveyed to Richard Bishop of Winchester 'all his lands tenements and hereditaments' in Cobham, Ockham, East Horsley and Walton on Thames.[18] No further description of the property is given, save that it had formerly been held by 'Aubrey, widow of Edmund'. The grant probably related to land at nearby Chilbrook and was made in connection with the Bishop's foundation of Corpus Christi College, Oxford.

3

ROYAL SERVANTS

A survey of the Manor of Cobham records that, in the first half of the 16th century, John Carleton held the lands 'which were all once Robert Bardsey's of Kingston upon Thames'.[1] John Carleton, a lawyer, was from the Oxfordshire village of Brightwell Baldwin, where he had purchased the manor in 1500. His tomb can still be seen in the parish church there and the inscription on it describes Carleton as being of Walton on Thames.[2] His main residence seems to have been at the Burwood estate in Walton parish that he had purchased from Corpus Christi College, Oxford.[3] John came from good stock. His maternal grandmother was Margaret Culpepper, who was an aunt of Queen Katherine Howard. He married well, choosing as his spouse Joyce, a daughter of William Welbeck, Citizen and Haberdasher in London.[4] The family were well connected and one of John and Joyce's daughters, Jane, married Erasmus Gaynisford (Gainsford) of Crowhurst Place. Through the Gainsfords there was also a link with the Slyfields of Great Bookham.

In 1538 Carleton was appointed a receiver of the Court of Augmentations, a government department set up to receive monastic property after the Dissolution. A receiver usually resided in his district which, for Carleton, was Berkshire, Buckinghamshire and Oxfordshire, where his family estates lay. As a royal official his influence in the county would have been considerable. 'The receiver's office was endowed with neither patronage nor disciplinary authority. Locally his power was subtle and indirect. In revenue collection he could insist upon the immediate payment of a debt to the crown, grant convenient terms, or ignore it altogether.'[5] In Surrey Carleton also held property in Pyrford and Dorking.

It is not known whether Carleton obtained the Cobham lands direct from the Bardsey family. As an officer of the Court of Augmentations, he was, of course, well placed to hear about attractive estates that were coming onto the market. If, as seems likely, he was the same John Carleton who was collector of rents for Chertsey Abbey on its manors of Cobham and Bookham, he would have known the area well.[6] In 1538 Carleton had been granted lands at Chilbrook by Corpus Christi College which appear to be identical to those granted to the Bishop of Winchester by Peter Bardsey in 1522.[7] In the same year Corpus Christi had exchanged its lands in Walton on Thames with the Crown for the advowson of Warborough, Oxfordshire. This appears to have been part of a process of exchange of lands between the college and Crown that resulted from Henry VIII's acquisition of Hampton Court from Cardinal Wolsey.

After the king had acquired Hampton Court he created a 'chase' for hunting. This was a large area that could be stocked with deer where the king could indulge in one of his favourite pastimes.[8] The chase enclosed the whole of the parishes of East and West Molesey, Walton on Thames, Weybridge and parts of Esher and Cobham. It was created by an Act of 1539 in which John Carleton is mentioned as one of the 'free tenants' with land within the proposed chase.[9] The southern perimeter of the chase was the river Mole at Cobham. In purchasing Robert Bardsey's property, Carleton acquired land just outside the jurisdiction of the chase and the burdens and obligations placed upon it by the king.[10] The opportunity to acquire these lands, the income from which was used to support the chantry at Kingston, may well have arisen as a result of Carleton's appointment in 1545 as one of the commissioners to survey Surrey chantries prior to their abolition.[11] It was said that the commissioners did not fail to seize so good an opportunity for enriching themselves.

Carleton appears to have been busy collecting posts for himself at this time and, as a receiver of the Court of Augmentations, he was also in a position to secure local offices controlled by the Court, especially in the Home Counties. Only a few months after obtaining his receivership Carleton was appointed to the office of steward and woodward of the close, or Chase, of Hampton Court.[12] As already mentioned, the Chase of Hampton Court took in a number of Surrey parishes and, for those living within it, it was not only extremely inconvenient but also produced great hardship as the commons, meadows and pasture were taken in and stocked with deer. In 1548 the Privy Council received a petition made by 'many poor men of Cobham and neighbouring parishes' setting out their complaints. As a result John Carleton and William Godwin were instructed to undertake a survey of seven questions to be answered on oath by 24 of 'the most substantial and discreet men.' The results of the survey are not known but within the next 12 years it was considered uneconomic to renew the fence that enclosed the chase and the land was restored to its former use and the deer removed to Windsor.[13] Yet another post held by Carleton was that of Steward of Lands to the Dean and Chapter of Westminster Abbey where his brother Gerard was as a canon.[14]

Carleton had five sons. The eldest was Anthony (1530-75) who was the father of Sir Dudley Carleton, 1st Viscount Dorchester and English Ambassador to The Hague.[15] John's second son George (1532-90) became involved in the activities of a tightly knit group of puritan gentry in the Midlands which linked him with the famous puritan conspiracy of the Marprelate Tracts. The third son, Edward (1540-82), married Mary, a daughter of George Bigley who had purchased the manor of Cobham in the reign of Queen Mary, and one of their sons, Bigley (1572-1634), later purchased an estate in Cobham overlooking the river Mole which is now the site of Leigh Place.[16] Bigley Carlton's daughter, Mary, married Rowland Wilson, a parliamentarian army officer and politician and, after his death in 1650, she became the third wife of Bulstrode Whitelock, the lawyer and parliamentarian who is best remembered as the author of the 'Memorials of the English Affairs from the beginning of the reign of Charles I'. The will of Bigley's brother Edward (1562-1618), refers to his 'messuage of 24 acres called Fragges and another parcel of wood called Leechroyden'.[17] Fragges lay to the south of Groverscrofte and was later taken into Cobham Park.[18] John Carleton's remaining two sons were John, who died unmarried in Italy, and William about whom nothing is known. Other descendants of John were Edward Carleton who built the core of the present Carshalton House, Surrey and Elizabeth Carleton, mother of Sir John Vanbrugh the architect.

Bridgelands is next heard of in 1581 when, in his will dated 16 March, John Hemyngway of Cobham, gentleman, bequeathed all his 'lands and tenements called or known by the name of Bridgelands, Chilbrook and Haywood' in Cobham, together with his lands in 'Stokedawburne', to his son-in-law Henry Besbeche and Elizabeth his wife 'my daughter'. The will was proved in 1582.[19]

Hemingway is first heard of in Cobham in 1566 when he purchased an acre of land at Street Cobham from George Carleton.[20] He is almost certainly the same John Hemingway who was an apothecary to Elizabeth I in 1558.[21] Hemingway's will reveals that he was a man of some substance. In addition to the Cobham estate he held the lease of a house in Long Woolstaple, Westminster which would have been very convenient for any duties at the royal court. This leasehold property, together with his best gown, was left to his nephew Edward.[22] To his cousin 'Bircheade', John left his velvet coat and 'a guilte cuppe with a cover fashioned like an arrow.' Guilt cups, bowls and spoons were bequeathed to various family members and his goddaughter, Elizabeth Sutton, who was almost certainly a member of the Cobham family of that name, received a silver spoon.

Hemingway does not appear to have had any sons and, as previously mentioned, he left his Cobham estates to his son-in-law and daughter Henry and Elizabeth Besbeche of Killingworth, Warwickshire. Besbeche was Steward to Robert Dudley, Earl of Leicester, once the great favourite of Elizabeth I, and it seems likely that Besbeche and Hemingway met through the Royal Court.[23] Henry and Elizabeth Besbeche did not hold the Cobham lands for long and in 1584 they granted the Chilbrook property to Robert Gavell of Cobham, lord of the manor.[24] This grant does not mention Bridgelands which may have been conveyed separately to Gavell. On 26 September 1585 Gavell sold to Thomas Hemingway 'all that Capitall Messuage or Tenement called or known by the name of Bridgelands' on the east side of the road leading to Horsley together with 26 acres of adjoining land. In addition there were one and half acres of land in 'Blackwater Meade', three acres in 'Woodye Meade' and ten acres in 'Ryefields'. 'Blackwater Meade' and 'Woodye Meade' were between the river Mole and Plough Lane in what are now called Plough Meadows. 'Ryefields' lay further south, close to Chilbrook Farm. Hemingway's purchase also included the 40 acres of land at Chilbrook together with Heywood on Cobham Fairmile, and a 20-acre holding called 'Bull Rydon' which lay next to the parish boundary with East Horsley.[25] The relationship of this Thomas Hemingway to John is not known and he is not referred to in John's will.

In 1593 Thomas Hemingway's son, also called Thomas, married Joan Southland of Ealing and Thomas senior entered into a marriage settlement made with Joan's father William.[26] The property to be settled on the newlyweds was 'the capital messuage called Bridgelands and land'. To describe the property as a 'capital messuage' implies a house of some importance. It would have been a timber-framed building and probably stood close to the site of the present Cobham Park mansion.

In 1598 the noted surveyor and cartographer Ralph Agas made a survey of the manor of Cobham. Agas recorded that 'Thomas Hemingwaie holds freely and by charter of indenture dated the 7th year of the reign of Edward IV and made with the Lord Abbot of Chertsey and the monks there for a croft called Grovers containing one acre of enclosed land called Bridge Land and five acres called Brockforde in Dounefelde.' In other words, this is exactly the land described in the grant to Robert Bardsey made 125 years earlier. The entry also records that 'the tenement now built there and various enclosed lands lie near Dounefeld on the south side and the returning river on the north side, the east headland abuts against the said returning river and the west headland against the High Street.' Reference to 'the tenement now built there' implies that the newly married couple had rebuilt the old house purchased by Thomas Hemingway senior in 1585 and this was almost certainly the property which became known as 'Bridge House Farm' and which was the predecessor of the first Cobham Park mansion. Agas also recorded Hemingway's other lands in the fields now known as Plough Meadows.

In 1613 Thomas Hemingway of Cobham, 'innholder', died and was buried in the churchyard of St Margaret, the parish church of Westminster that stands next to the great Abbey. His burial in Westminster seems to link him back to John Hemingway who had a property in Long Woolstaple there. The fact that this Thomas was described as an innholder suggests that he had taken up residence at the *Swan* in Street Cobham leaving his son and daughter-in-law to enjoy Bridgelands. Thomas's will refers to his wife Mary and his sons John, Robert and Thomas. John the youngest son was to have all his father's freehold land in Cobham when he was 21 years old, and his eldest son Thomas was to have his lands in Brentford. Nothing further is heard of the Cobham lands until 20 August 1634 when John and Jane Hemyngway of Whitechapel and Thomas and Katherine Hemyngway of Norton Folgate (a street in the Bishopsgate area of London), sold the 'capital Messuage or Tenement called or known by the name of Bridgelands' together with 'Blackwater Meade', 'Woody Meade' and 'Ryefields' to Symon Walter of Little Bookham, 'Gentleman' for £500.[27]

At the time of the sale to Symon Walter, Thomas Sutton occupied Bridgelands.[28] Thomas was descended from Richard Sutton who leased the manor of Cobham from Chertsey Abbey.[29] Richard's widow, Elizabeth, married George Bigley and it was their daughter, Mary, who married John Carleton's son Edward. Mary Bigley's sister, Dorothy, who inherited the manor of Cobham, married Robert Gavell. The Gavells and the Suttons emerge as important gentry families in Cobham in the 16th and 17th centuries. Thomas Sutton was the impropriator of the living of Cobham and received the rectorial income. Bridgelands appears to have been his chief residence at this time.

In 1640 Thomas Sutton and John Hemingway were involved in a legal action which reached the ears of Charles I. A petition submitted on behalf of Hemingway stated that, Sutton 'being Tenant to the Land in question did for divers yeares in the minority of the petitioner solicit and importune him to take money of him for his unnecessary expense.' In other words Sutton was loaning money to Hemingway which was to be repaid upon his obtaining his majority. However, the petition reveals that after the Cobham estate had been sold, Hemingway had left for the West Indies and in his absence Sutton sued for monies owed. When Hemingway returned from overseas and 'before hee could proceed in Equity hee was cast into prison'. The petition goes on to relate that Symon Walter had sold the land for perhaps as much as £1,300. The outcome of this episode is not known and we are left to guess whether Sutton was the villain of the piece or whether Hemingway had been living beyond his means.[30]

In 1650 Sutton figured in the episode of Gerrard Winstanley and the Diggers. When the Diggers moved from St George's Hill, Weybridge to the Little Heath at Cobham, it was Sutton, together with John Platt, lord of the manor, who instigated the destruction of their settlement there and drove them from the parish. On 30 May 1631 the Cobham Churchwarden's Book lists Cobham property owners and their responsibilities for the upkeep and maintenance of the church 'paynes' or fence. The list, which was updated later in the century, records, 'Mr Sutton for Hemingwaies land now Mr Carpenter – the style gate.' Responsibility for the 'style gate' as opposed to one or two individual 'paynes' indicates the importance of this property. 'Mr Carpenter', the later owner, was William Carpenter, of whom more in the following chapter.

4

THE KING'S FRIEND

What happened to the Hemingways after the sale of Bridgelands is not known. Neither is it clear who held the lands that were to become Cobham Park during the unsettled years of the civil war and the Interregnum which followed. No further reference can be found to Symon Walter of Little Bookham who purchased the property in 1634 and it is not until the closing years of the 17th century that we find documentary evidence relating to these lands. In 1693 Robert Gavell, lord of the manor of Cobham, mortgaged to Robert Corffe a property described as follows:

> All That Messuage or Tenement and farm together with the Barns Stables Edifices and Buildings Gardens Orchards and Backsides thereto belonging … containing in the whole by estimation 30 acres (be the same more or less) situate lying and being in Cobham aforesaid and called or known by the name of Bridge Lands or by whatever other name or names the same or any part or parcel thereof was called or known and then or then late in the Tenure or Occupation of the said Robert Gavell his assigns or undertenants and were the Messuage and Lands of William Carpenter deceased and in the occupation of the said William Carpenter or his assigns and afterwards in the occupation of Margaret Carpenter Widow deceased and were purchased by the said Robert Gavell of Caleb Westbrook then late of Kingston upon Thames.[1]

Once again this property corresponds to the former property of Thomas Hemingway and Robert Bardsey.

Robert Gavell was the son of Vincent Gavell and Margaret Lynde and a great grandson of Robert Gavell and Dorothy Bigley (see p.10).[2] Vincent died not long after the birth of Robert and Margaret married again, to John Platt minister of West Horsley who became one of the chief players in the episode of Gerrard Winstanley and the Diggers. Robert married his cousin Elizabeth Lynde of Rickmansworth and, in due course, he acquired the manor of Cobham and Cobham Court from his mother and stepfather. Presumably the Gavells chose to live at Cobham Court after their marriage. According to the 1693 mortgage Gavell had purchased Bridgelands from Caleb Westbrooke of Kingston upon Thames. As will be seen, Westbrooke was the lawyer for the previous owner, William Carpenter.

William Carpenter was an important man and appears to have been close to Charles II. He was described as one of the 'gentlemen of his majestys privye chamber extraordinary'.[3] When the restoration of the monarchy in 1660 prompted Parliament to ask the nation to make a 'free and voluntary present' to the King, the largest donor in Cobham, and one of the largest in Surrey, was William Carpenter who donated the substantial sum of £5. In 1662 he was elected High Constable of Elmbridge 'in the roome and stead of George Smithier'.[4] In 1663 Carpenter was granted a coat of arms.[5] The greyhound on his arms might refer to his role as a King's Messenger. He was probably the same William Carpenter who, in 1666, was appointed Deputy Keeper of the Privy Lodgings and Standing Wardrobe at Greenwich where Charles II was building a new palace. Carpenter was also 'Groom of the Hunting and Padd Stable'.[6]

The Surrey Hearth Tax returns of 1664 list 'Mr Carpenter' as being chargeable for nine hearths, making Bridge House Farm one of the largest houses in Cobham, eclipsed only by Cobham Court which had 13 hearths and Downe Place and *The White Lion* inn, each of which had eleven. Adjoining the house was a rabbit warren and, in 1664, it is recorded that 'Richard Crowcher or Crutcher of Walton on Thames, warrener and husbandman, stole a coney hutch trap from William Carpenter of Cobham'.[7]

William Carpenter died in 1672 and was buried in Cobham church, where part of the slab covering his tomb can just be seen on the floor of the north chapel.[8] Following his death a full inventory of 'the goods chattels and householdstuffe' was made by a Mr Millward and Caleb Westbrooke who is referred to in the 1693 mortgage by Robert Gavell. This fascinating document has survived and, in the absence of any drawings or painting of Bridge House Farm, is the next best thing. It describes the contents of the house room by room giving the value of each item listed and clearly conveys the wealth of Carpenter.[9]

Bridge House Farm had nine rooms and a dairy. On the upper floor there was 'the Chamber over the Hall' which had two beds, three chests, a table, cupboard, stool and two chairs. This was obviously the master bedroom and was decorated with 'hangings' and two mirrors. In 'the Chamber over the Little Parlour' there were one bed, six chairs, six stools, a table and a cupboard. Both these rooms had fireplaces. The 'Maides Chamber' contained one bed together with a table and trunk. The 'Chamber over the Kitchen' had one bed, one table, two chairs, two stools, and a chest, a carpet and window curtains. It also had a fireplace. Next to this was the 'Mans Chamber', which contained two beds. On the ground floor the house had a 'Great Parlour', which had a 'small and great table with carpets', a dozen chairs, six pictures and the necessary items for the fireplace. The 'Little Parlour' had two tables, seven chairs, a form, a cupboard, four cushions, hangings and, again, the necessary fireplace items. There was a Hall which contained two tables, ten stools, six cushions, two chairs and a clock. The kitchen was well equipped with 22 pewter dishes, two dozen plates, five candlesticks, a flagon, six saucers, three chamber pots, two basins, a stewing pan and tin utensils. There were also various brass utensils, a musket, a fowling piece, chairs, stools and other lumber. The Dairy was an essential part of the household and this contained all the necessary equipment. The outhouses contained wood and coal. Carpenter was wealthy enough to keep his own coach and harness. Elsewhere there were three cows, one horse, two hogs, five pigs, poultry, hay in the barn, corn in the granary and last, but by no means least, 'Doung in the yard'. The total value of the contents including 'his apparel and money in his purse' and debts owing to him were £339.

In his will, William Carpenter refers to his daughter-in-law 'Elizabeth the wife of John Covert'. This seems to imply that Elizabeth may have been the child of a first marriage of Carpenter's wife Margaret. In her will, dated 9 July 1675, Margaret Carpenter left to her granddaughter Margaret Covert 'at marriage or when she is 21' all her property called 'Bottles' which she had 'late bought' of Sir Francis Vincent.[10] 'Bottles' appears to have stood close to the site of Cobham Lodge in Cobham Park Road with lands dispersed around it. In 1742 'Bottles' became part of Cobham Park and its history is told in the following chapter. The Covert family are known to have been living at Bottles in the early 18th century.

In 1708 Robert Gavell senior, together with his son Robert junior, sold the manor of Cobham and several farms, including Bridgelands, to Frances, Viscountess Lanesborough, reserving to themselves Cobham Court and the farm attached to it. Cobham Court had been home of the manorial bailiffs under Chertsey Abbey and was the place where the manorial court was held. When the manor of Cobham was sold into private hands, Cobham Court became the manor house.[11]

Frances Lanesborough was the daughter of the Dowager Viscountess Lanesborough. In 1691 Frances, as a considerable heiress, had married Henry Fox, a wealthy Yorkshire gentleman. Frances's father, George Lane, owned estates in county Roscommon, Ireland and had served the future King Charles II during his years of exile. He had been knighted at Bruges in 1657 and was created Viscount Lanesborough in 1676, taking his title from a manor in county Longford which he had been granted in 1664. George Lane was married three times, his third wife being Frances Sackville, daughter of the 5th Earl of Dorset. When Lord Lanesborough died in 1683 his widow married Denny Muschamp, who then owned Bishop's Manor in East Horsley. Denny's brother, Ambrose, owned the other two manors in East Horsley. Following the death of her husband and brother-in-law, Lady Lanesborough acquired all three East Horsley manors.

When Lady Lanesborough died in 1721 she left the manor of Cobham and Bridge House Farm to her grandson, James Fox, and with this opened a new chapter in the history of the lands that were to become Cobham Park.

5

'A BEAUTIFUL HOUSE'

In 1728 Lady Lanesborough's grandson James Fox sold Bridge House Farm to John Bridges for £1,000. Until recently John Bridges remained a mysterious figure about whom little was known. However, new research has revealed that he was a member of a prolific Warwickshire family whose ancestry can be traced back to the 16th century. John's father was Sir Brook Bridges (1643-1717), who had been both Auditor of the Imprest, a lucrative and prestigious post in the Treasury, and one of the first Directors of the Bank of England. Sir Brook's father had been the Parliamentarian Colonel John Bridges of Alcester, Governor of Warwick Castle during the Civil War.[1]

John, born in about 1682, was Sir Brook's second son. He was probably brought up at his father's residence 'Grove House' in Fulham, which was then a pleasant village on the outskirts of London. Sir Brook retired from his post at the Treasury in 1705 and settled at Goodnestone near Wing in Kent, where he built an imposing new mansion. John is said to have later recorded that his father 'having been blessed with a plentiful fortune he purchased an estate in this parish, when having repaired and adorned the church and having caused to be erected a mansion house for his family he departed this life on the 18th day of December 1717.' Following Sir Brook's death, the Goodnestone estate passed to John's elder brother, also named Brook, and the family continued there until the 19th century. However, had John's nephew, the 2nd baronet, died childless his will stipulated that all his estates at Goodnestone and elsewhere in Kent were to pass to 'my loving uncle John Bridges Esq. and to his heirs and assigns for ever'.[2]

Little is known of John Bridges' early life. He may have been the 'John Bridges, of the Inner Temple, Esq.' who is listed as one of the subscribers to Harris's *History of Kent* published in 1719, and a 1721 copy of Richard Bradley's *Works of Nature* from the Cobham Park library lists a 'John Bridges of Soho Square' as a subscriber. Parish Rate Books record an Elizabeth Bridges at 10 Soho Square at this time. Elizabeth Bridges, 'Spinster of St Anne's, Westminster', had leased the property from the Earl of Berkeley in 1716.[3] She was a niece of Colonel John Bridges of Alcester and her brother William was MP for Liskeard and Surveyor of the Ordnance at the Tower of London. When William died in 1714 he left his entire estate to Elizabeth including at least £4,000 in bank stock. When Elizabeth died she left the manor of Wallington, Surrey to her great nephew, Sir Brook Bridges, 3rd baronet of Goodnestone.

When John's father Sir Brook made his will in December 1717 he left all his estates in Fulham and Kent to his elder son. John, the younger son, was not overlooked.[4] Sir Brook's will stated that he had already made over annuities to John in 1702 and 1706 amounting to £50 per annum and £40 per annum respectively.[5] Furthermore Sir Brook had settled an estate of £400 per annum upon John and 'Mrs Anne Lewyn' by their Marriage Articles dated 18 October 1716.[6] This sum was settled upon the understanding that John and Anne would continue to live with Sir Brook who had been widowed some years before. The will provided for a further sum of £400 per annum to be settled upon John and Ann at Sir Brook's death. To provide this income, Sir Brook left a capital sum of £10,000 to be invested and administered by John's brother.[7] When his brother died in 1727, the capital sum of £10,000 was released to John. Amongst the other legacies in Sir Brook's will were the sum of £100 to Christ's Hospital, of which he was a Governor, and £100 to be divided among four charity schools in St Clement Danes, St Margaret Westminster, the parish of Fulham and the city of Canterbury. A further sum of £50 was to be distributed 'to those not receiving alms either in London or elsewhere'. Sir Brook's 'plate, books, household goods, coaches and horses' were to be divided between his two sons.

It is not known for certain why John Bridges chose Cobham as his home. He may have known the area through his relations at Wallington or through his father's cousin who had married Richard Rooth of Epsom.[8] However, it now seems more than likely that John had been introduced to James Fox, the owner of the Cobham estate, by a distant relative. Fox was in Italy in 1725-7 as part of the Grand Tour and is reported to have travelled with a John Bridges. This is unlikely to have been John Bridges of Cobham as he was several years older than Fox. It has been suggested that Fox's travelling companion was the son of William Bridges of Covent Garden.[9] Whoever he was, he was almost certainly related to John Bridges of Cobham and that it was he who introduced John to James Fox.

The agreement and purchase deeds for Bridge House Farm describe John Bridges as being 'of Cobham' which suggests that he was already living in the parish. No other references to him being in Cobham have been found except for one intriguing document – a policy for the insurance of Church Stile House issued by the Sun Insurance Company in November 1725.[10] That property was then owned by the parish of Clerkenwell in London but leased by Robert Porter, who took out the insurance. The policy refers to part of the property being tenanted by 'Mr Bridges'. The part of the building occupied by this Mr Bridges appears to have been the brick wing added at the rear sometime early in the 18th century. In 1938 the Clerk to the Clerkenwell Charity Trustees wrote that 'the other house at the back was probably built under a building lease granted in 1726'.[11] Unfortunately that lease, together with other deeds, can no longer be traced. However, it is interesting to speculate whether the Mr Bridges recorded on the insurance policy was the John Bridges who purchased Bridge House Farm and even further to speculate whether it was he who had built the addition to Church Stile House.

No doubt John Bridges wished to invest his recent inheritance soundly in an estate befitting his financial status and Bridge House Farm and its lands provided him with an opportunity to create such an estate. However, before the sale could take place James Fox was required to obtain an Act of Parliament varying the terms of his grandmother's will. In this Act Bridge House Farm was described as 'a very old House and Out-Houses frequently out of Repair' which had, for many years, been let to Jeremiah Freeland and Richard Luff.[12]

Bridges wasted no time in demolishing the old house and replacing it with a splendid new classical mansion built in the latest fashionable style. John Bridges' choice of architect is not recorded but it is now believed by architectural historians that he chose Roger Morris, a close friend and associate of Lord Burlington of Chiswick House, and an early exponent of the Palladian style. The Cobham house with its octagonal cupola atop a pyramidal roof is exactly the same as those at Combe House (1725), White Lodge in Richmond Park (from 1727), South Dalton House in Yorkshire, and Westcombe House in Kent (1730), all of which are known to be by or attributed to Roger Morris.[13] In his book on Palladio's houses in the Veneto, Witold Rybcznski writes, 'It is always interesting to speculate how a client chooses an architect, whether by a social connection, a recommendation, or a chance encounter.'[14] All three might have applied, as Morris was Bridges' neighbour for a while when he lived at Green Street, near Soho Square, and was designing houses for clients in the newly laid out Grosvenor Square.

John Bridges' house was one of the grandest in the district and could be seen from a distance of some miles away. Two scraps of paper with the Fox family papers in the Surrey History Centre contain a sketch plan with the dimensions of the ground-floor rooms and the following description of the house:

> Mr Bridges house at Cobham is very much after the Modell of Sig. Marco Zeno's No. 35 in ye 3d Book of Palladio as to the South Front & the North: except that the Door has some ornament sch. Zeno's has not; and that the semi circular window wch. In Zeno's is placed between the 2 rows of windows & gives light into the Hall, is in Mr Bridges' sett in the upper two; by wch means the rooms over the vestibule at Mr Bridges' has no window, nor light, unless from the semi circular window on the Story above it. In the Middle there is a Turret that gives light to the passages in the First Story where are the Mezzanines, wch are over all the rooms except the Salloon & Drawing room as under. On the E. and W. Front are square windows to the Mezzanini, wch with ye rooms beneath are 20 Feet as the Dr: & Salln., over them is a 10 Foot Story light by the upper row of windows and the Passages by the Turrett – over these are 4 rooms for servts.[15]

There is no date on either of the two scraps but as they were filed with other family papers dated between 1737 and 1741 it is likely they date from this period. But why did Fox require this information? It is tempting to link it with work which he was having carried out at his then principal residence of East Horsley Place, just four miles or so from Cobham. Fox had inherited an old house which he modernised in the 1750s. Contemporary drawings of that place show a large Venetian window as having been added to the old hall in the centre of the building. Venetian windows were very much the trademark of the Burlington circle. Had Fox requested the description of the Cobham house because he was contemplating something similar for himself in East Horsley?

John Bridges' name cannot be found in any local parish or manorial records except in reference to his land acquisitions. However, there is one intriguing reference to him in the Surrey Quarter Sessions records for 1732, when John Bridges and William Bellamy Esquires were presented 'for digging and carrying away gravel or causing so as to be done whereby a pitt is made dangerous to His Majesty's liege subjects passing that way adjoining to the road leading from Street Cobham to Esher'.[16] Bellamy, a wealthy barrister, was the owner of the Painshill estate immediately prior to the Hon. Charles Hamilton, who created the famous landscape park there. Presumably both Bridges and Bellamy required gravel for building work – possibly for use in their parks. It is inconceivable that two wealthy neighbouring landowners, such as Bridges and Bellamy, would not have known one another. Perhaps it was Bellamy who introduced Bridges to Cobham. As educated men of fashion they must surely have exchanged ideas concerning the building of their houses and the creation of the surrounding parkland.

On 4 December 1736 John Bridges married Mary Western, the wealthy widow of Thomas Western of Rivenhall, Essex. The marriage took place at Oxford Chapel (now St Peter's), Vere Street in London. Mary Western was the daughter of Sir Richard Shirley of Preston in Sussex. Mary's first husband, Thomas Western, had died in 1733 and their son, also named Thomas, was twice painted by William Hogarth. The second picture is a family conversation piece painted in about 1736 to mark his marriage the previous year. The painting includes friends and relatives together with Thomas's widowed mother who was then on the eve of her marriage to John Bridges. It is possible that Mary and her new husband were also painted by Hogarth but the whereabouts of this painting (if it exists) is not known.[17] Nothing is known of the lives of John and Mary at Cobham although they continued to maintain Mary's London house in fashionable George Street, off Hanover Square.

Samuel Richardson's augmented version of Daniel Defoe's *A Tour Through The Whole Island of Great Britain* has the following description of John Bridges' house and gardens:

> Near this Place [Cobham] is the House of Mr Bridges, which is built in a very singular Taste, something after the Model of an Italian Villa, but very plain on the outside. The Apartments within seem very commodious, and the principal rooms are elegantly fitted up, the Ceilings being gilt, and all the Members are richly ornamented. The Offices below are very convenient, and judiciously contrived to answer the purposes for which they were designed. But what chiefly struck my Curiosity on seeing it, was a false Story contrived on each side of the house, taken from the Difference in the Height of the Side-Rooms, from those principal

Apartments at one end; and these are converted into long galleries with a small Apartment at one end, which affords a Communication between them. In the Attick Story there are very good Lodging-rooms, which are well laid together so that for the size of this House, there is hardly any near London, which has more useful and elegant Apartments.

Of the surroundings, Richardson writes that the river Mole which bordered the estate had been widened to four or five times its original width and the excavated soil used to create 'a natural slope, with a broad Grass-walk, planted with sweet Shrubs on each side; and at the End of the Walk is a fine Room, which has a view of the Water lengthwise, and is a sweet retreat in hot Weather, being shaded by large Elm-trees on the South-side, and having the water on the North and East-sides, which renders it very cool and pleasant.'

It is interesting to speculate whether, if Bridges were landscaping his property, William Bellamy was involved in similar work at Painshill? If so, this might call into question Horace Walpole's statement that Charles Hamilton had made his park out of 'a most cursed hill'. Perhaps Charles Hamilton's work was more of an adaptation of an existing and more formalised garden created by Bellamy.

In 1754 Dr Richard Pococke came to look at the house which he afterwards described as 'a beautiful house & there is something very curious in the contrivance of having two stories in some part of the house and one in another part'.[18]

Bridge House Farm was surrounded by various small copyhold holdings, none of which amounted to much more than a few acres, and these Bridges set about purchasing from his neighbours so that he could create a park fitting for his new house. A more substantial addition was made to the estate in 1742 when Bridges purchased the property known as 'Bottells' from Samuel Aldridge, a draper from Thame in Oxfordshire.[19] 'Bottells' comprised about forty acres of land to the south of Bridge House Farm.[20] In 1743 Bridges purchased 6¾ acres of land from Lancelot Barrett. This comprised three-quarters of an acre in East Field, five acres in 'Upper and Lower Ansteds' and one acre of coppice.[21] The five acres corresponds with the five acres called 'Broksere' referred to in the grant to Robert Bardsey.

After his second wife's death John seems to have lost interest in his Cobham estate. Perhaps it held too many happy but sad memories for him and on 20th March 1749 he sold it to The Rt. Hon. Sir John Ligonier, Commander in Chief of the British Army. The sale price was £6,500. The property was described as 'the Capital Messuage or Mansion House lately erected and built thereon by the said John Bridges'.[22] Before completing the transaction another Act of Parliament was required to confirm an agreement which Bridges had entered into with James Fox for the exchange of various small parcels of land, amounting in total to about four and a half acres. There appears to have been some uncertainty as to Bridges' title to what had been Bridge House Farm and so on 17 May 1748 he entered into a deed with George Fox of Bramham Park in Yorkshire to confirm the original purchase and 'for obviating and removing all doubts controversies and disputes that have arisen or may arise'.[23]

After the sale John Bridges returned to London. The 1749 Poll Book for Westminster records him as having a residence at George Street and in 1762 he made his last will from that address stipulating that he should be buried 'in the family vault at Goodnestone by my dear late wife'.[24] John's will reveals that he was a generous man warmly disposed to remember acts of kindness. Most of his servants benefited under his will and to his housekeeper he left the sum of £100 'in consideration of the care she took of her Mistress during her last illness'. The residue of the estate was left to his great nephew Sir Brook Bridges, the 3rd baronet. Sir Brook's children were also remembered by their great-great uncle, including Elizabeth who later married Edward Knight, the brother of Jane Austen. The novelist's letters often referred to her cousins of the Bridges family whom she visited at Goodnestone and it has been suggested that the house was the model for the home of Lady Catherine de Burgh in *Pride and Prejudice*.

1 All Saints' Parish Church, Kingston upon Thames, 1800. Robert Bardsey, 'citizen and fishmonger of London', and the earliest known owner of the land which became Cobham Park, was granted letters patent for the foundation of a religious fraternity of the Holy Spirit in All Saints in 1477. It is possible that he is buried in the chapel but no monument has survived.

2 The seal of Chertsey Abbey, Lords of the Manor of Cobham, who granted an estate at Cobham to Robert Bardsey in recognition of his 'faithful services and counsels'.

3 St Bartholomew's church at Brightwell Baldwin, Oxfordshire. The final resting place of John Carleton who acquired the Cobham lands in c.1540.

4 Tomb of John Carleton, St Bartholomew's, Brightwell Baldwin.

5 The inscription on the tomb of John Carleton reads 'Here resteth the bodyes of John Carlton Esquier & Joyce his wife wch John was ye first name owner & lorde of this towne & came from Walton apon Thames in ye countie of Surie – they had issue V sons as Antony, George, Willim, John, John dyed unmarried at Bolonia De-gracia in Itali, & Edwarde. Daughter IIII as Anne married to Rowland Lytton, Katelin to Francis Blunte esq brother to ye Lord Monjoy, and Jane married to Erasmus Gainsford esquire.'

6 In 1640 John Hemingway of Cobham petitioned the Privy Council in an action against Thomas Sutton who was the tenant of the estate at Cobham. This document is now preserved in the House of Lords Records Office.

An ACT to enable James Fox Esq; and others, to make Leases of the Estate in the County of Surrey, devised to the said James Fox by Frances late Viscountess Lanesborough, and for Sale of Bridge-house Farm, part of the said Estate, and Investing the Money in the Purchase of other Lands in the same County, to be settled to the like Uses; and for other Purposes therein mentioned.

WHEREAS Frances Viscountess Dowager Lanesborough, in the Kingdom of Ireland, did, on or about the Eighth of December, in the Year of our Lord One thousand seven hundred and nineteen, duly Sign, Seal and Publish her last Will and Testament in Writing, and thereby amongst other Things gave and devised all her Mannors, Messuages, Lands, Tenements and Hereditaments, as well Freehold as Copyhold, lying and being in the County of Surrey, to her second Grandson James Fox, then of Christ-Church Colledge in Oxford, for and during the Term of his natural Life; and after the Determination of his Estate for Life therein, she gave and devised the same to Richard Turner of the Inner-Temple, London, Esq; and William Dawsor of Leather-head in the said County of Surrey Esq; and their Heirs, during the Life of the said James Fox, for preserving the contingent Remainders therein after mentioned : And from and after the Decease of the said James Fox, she devised the same to the first, and all other the Sons of the said James Fox severally and successively according to Seniority, and the Heirs Male of their respective Bodies issuing, the Elder thereof and his Heirs Male being first preferred to take; and for want of such Issue, she gave and devised the said Mannors, Messuages, Lands, Tenements and Hereditaments to Sackville Fox, her third Grandson, for and during the Term of his natural Life, with Remainder to the same Trustees to preserve contingent Remainders, with Remainder to his the said Sackville Fox's first and every other Son in Tail Male successively, with Remainder to George Fox, her eldest Grandson, for and during the Term of his Natural Life, with Remainder to the same Trustees to preserve contingent Remainders, Remainder to the said George Fox's first and every other Son in Tail Male successively, with Remainder to the said Viscountess Lanesborough's own right Heirs for ever, subject to a Proviso, That in Case the said James Fox should not, within seven Years after her Decease enter into Holy Orders of Priesthood, then and immediately from and after the end of the said seven Years to be reckoned from her Death, the Rents and Profits of the Estate thereby devised to him, should during his Life be paid to and distributed among all her younger Grand-children, in equal Parts, until he should enter into such Orders; and if he should enter into such Orders, then and from thenceforth he should have the Rents and Profits that should grow due himself, as by the said Will, relation being thereunto had, doth and may more fully appear.

And whereas the said Frances Viscountess Lanesborough soon after died, without revoking the said Will, after whose Death the said James Fox entered upon the said Premisses so devised to him.

And whereas the said Mannors, Messuages, Lands, Tenements and Hereditaments and Premisses so devised to the said James Fox, have been usually let in Lease, and were so at the Time of the Death of the said Viscountess Lanesborough, some of which are now expired, and many of the rest will expire soon.

And whereas the said James Fox is only Tenant for Life by the said Will, and has not any Power given him thereby, to lett any Lease or Leases of the said Mannors, Messuages, Lands, Tenements and Hereditaments and Premisses, or of any part of them, to continue longer than his own Life, by which Omission or want of Power the Premisses can't be improved to the best Advantage, unless they are granted for a certain Term; which Defect or want of Power can't be effectually supplyed without the Aid of an Act of Parliament.

AND

7 The tomb of William Carpenter at St Andrew's church, Cobham is now partly obscured by choir stalls installed in the 19th century. Carpenter lived at Bridge House Farm at the end of the 17th century. Bridge House Farm was demolished in the 1730s and replaced by the first Cobham Park mansion.

8 (above right) Title page from an Act of Parliament made in 1728 to allow James Fox to sell Bridge Farm to John Bridges.

9 Cobham Park, south front, c.1810 by William Porden. Although made some seventy years after the house was built, this and the subsequent drawing show the house much as it would have appeared in the time of John Bridges.

10   Cobham Park, north front, c.1810 by William Porden.

11   This painting by William Hogarth is believed to show Thomas Western of Rivenhall, Essex leading by the hand his wife Anne Callis whom he married in 1735/6. He is showing a bird to his mother, Mary Shirley, widow of Thomas Western MP (1693-1733), who later married John Bridges who built the first Cobham Park mansion. The clergyman beside her is thought to be Archdeacon Charles Plumptre. Hogarth is believed to have painted two companion portraits of John and Mary Bridges but these cannot be traced.

12   Sketch of floor plan and brief description of Cobham Park in c.1740. This was made for James Fox, the previous owner of the Cobham estate. Fox was remodelling his own house at East Horsley and may have been getting ideas from the new house at Cobham.

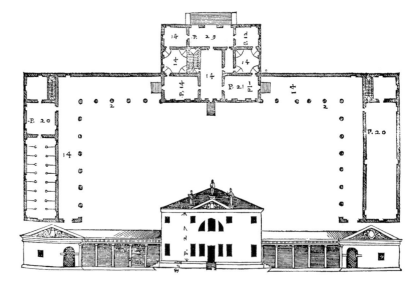

13 Villa Zeno by Palladio. According to the note made for James Fox, John Bridges' house at Cobham was based on the design of Andrea Palladio's Venetian villa.

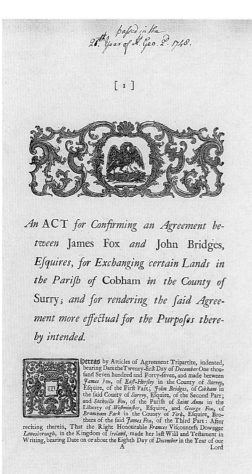

An ACT for *Confirming an Agreement between* James Fox *and* John Bridges, *Esquires, for Exchanging certain Lands in the Parish of* Cobham *in the County of* Surry; *and for rendering the said Agreement more effectual for the Purposes thereby intended.*

14 (left)   An Act of Parliament was required in 1748 to clarify the various land exchanges made between James Fox and John Bridges. This was done to enable Bridges to proceed with his sale of the estate to Lord Ligonier.

15 (above)   Field Marshal Lord Ligonier (1702-70) from the portrait by Sir Joshua Reynolds.

16 (left) This extract from John Rocque's map of Surrey, published in the middle of the 18th century, shows the extent of Cobham Park at the time of Ligonier.

17 (above) Coat of Arms of the Downe family. William de la Dune was Keeper of the King's Hanaper. Edward I appears to have made several visits to the house when passing through Surrey.

18 Down Farm. This aerial view shows what is believed to be the remains of a moat that partly surrounds the building. Lord Ligonier purchased Down Farm in 1759 and added it to the Cobham Park estate. It remains the Home Farm.

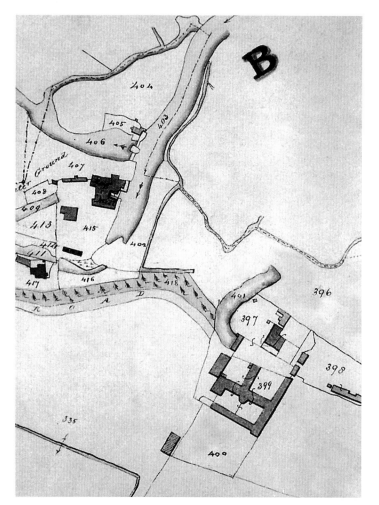

19 Down Farm (1839). The curved pond is believed to be the remnants of an ornamental moat. Downside Mill is to the north-west of the farmhouse.

20 A team from the Surrey Archaeological Society carried out an excavation at Down Farm, site of the former Downe Hall or Place, in 2004. The resulting evidence seems to establish that the site has been occupied for at least one thousand years.

21 (above)   Edward, Lord Ligonier in 1770 from the portrait by Thomas Gainsborough.

22 (above right)   Lady Penelope Ligonier in 1770 from the portrait by Thomas Gainsborough.

23 (right)   Count Vittorio Alfieri whose affair with Penelope Ligonier at Cobham Park led to a public scandal, a private duel with Lord Ligonier and eventual divorce.

24 'The Diabolady', 1777. This caricature shows a number of notorious 18th-century ladies applying to be Queen of Hell to Lord Irnham, who is depicted as the Devil. Lady Ligonier is on the far left holding a piece of paper on which is written 'Countess and the Stable Boy'. This alludes to her affair with a stable boy at Cobham Park.

25 'The Stable Adventure, or the Luckey Expedient.' This is another caricature of Lady Ligonier's affair with a stable boy at Cobham Park. Here Lady Ligonier encourages her sister to take a ride on a horse so that she can be alone with Thomas Johnson who is seen lurking behind the stall.

26   Edmund Malone (1741-1812), the great Shake-spearean scholar, rented Cobham Park for a short spell in 1788.

27 James Boswell, the biographer of Samuel Johnson, visited his friend Malone at Cobham Park and stayed overnight.

28   The Rev. Dr John Trusler, eccentric entre-preneurial clergyman who rented a small farm on the Cobham Park estate in the 1770s. Here he wrote his *Practical Husbandry*.

A Particular of the Mansion House Park and Estates
of the Heirs at Law of The Right Honourable Earl
Ligonier deceased called Cobham Park situate in the
Parish of Cobham in the County of Surry and who are
Richard Dawson Esq. Henry Charles Edward Vernon
Esq. an Infant and Francis Lloyd Esq.

Tenants Names	Premises	Quantity
		a r p
Alexander Raby Esq.	The Mansion House & Pleasure Grounds	20 " — " 13
Do	The Park Canal Meadow and Trustees Field	120 " 2 " 1
Do	The new Allotments on the late Inclosure	52 " — " 30
Do	The Farm of which there is a meadow called Bookham Meadow containing Two Acres and 55 Perches	121 " 3 " 11
Do	Cottage & Garden in field	" 0 " 26
Do	Another Cottage & Garden	" — " 23
Do	Two Tenements &c	" 2 " 35
Do	An Old Farm House & Garden	" 3 " 11
Richard Chasmer	An Allotment on the New Inclosure	16 " 2 " 19
Do	Farm	39 " 2 " 11
William Brown	Allotments on Do	34 " 2 " —
	Farm	00 " 3 " —
Revd Dr Trusler	House Garden & Meadow & New Allotments	14 " 1 " 21
John Goddard	Cottage & Garden	" — " 20
George Heel	Do	
Henry Hill	Do	" 1 " 5
John Tripper	A Meadow called Book Meadow	1 " — " 26
In hand	The Woods	20 " 2 " 17
Several Persons	The Tythes of several Estates amounting to	343 " 0 " 33

All which said Premises are occupied as follows — [turn over

29 This schedule of properties making up the Cobham Park estate was prepared in 1800 for the assessment of Land Tax. The Rev. Dr Trusler is shown as occupying a 'House Garden & Meadow & New Allotments' totalling 14a 1r 1p.

30 (above) Henry Lawes Luttrell, 2nd Earl of Carhampton (1743-1821). Carhampton purchased Cobham Park from Lord Ligonier's executors in 1801.

31 (above right) Jane Boyd, Countess Carhampton, one of the great beauties of her day.

32 (right) Carhampton was satirised by Gillray as 'The Irish Arithmetician proving 296 to be more than 1,143' after the Middlesex election of 1769. The radical John 'Liberty' Wilkes had gained 1,143 votes but was passed over in favour of the more acceptable Luttrell.

33 Harvey Christian Combe (1752-1818). This, together with the companion portrait of Alice Combe, was probably painted about the time of their marriage in 1780.

34 Alice Christian Combe, née Tree (1758-1828).

35 The former London home of Harvey Christian Combe at 100-2 Great Russell Street. Originally Thanet House, it was built about 1693, reputedly by Wren. In the late 18th century it was divided into two, the larger part being occupied by Combe. Here he entertained members of the Royal Family. The façade of the house was modernised in the 1820s. The house is now part of the complex of buildings that houses the Florida State University London Study Centre.

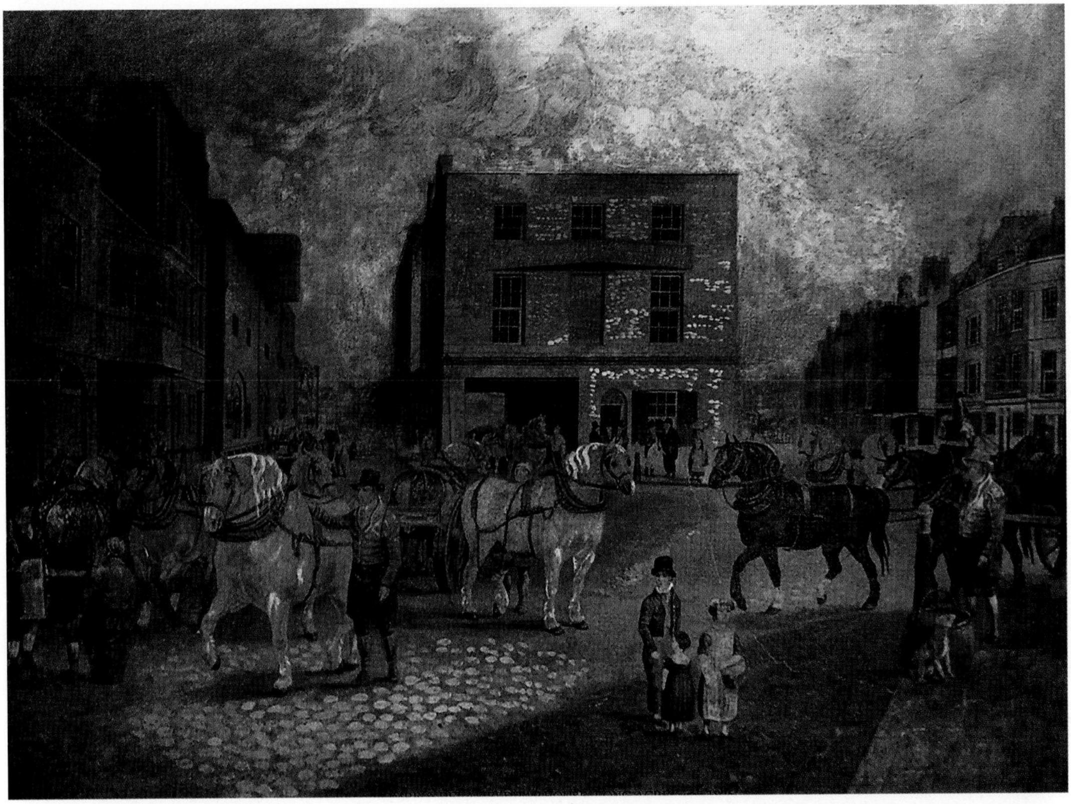

36 The Wood Yard Brewery, Castle Street, Longacre, London from an early 19th-century painting. Some of these buildings have survived and have been converted into fashionable boutiques.

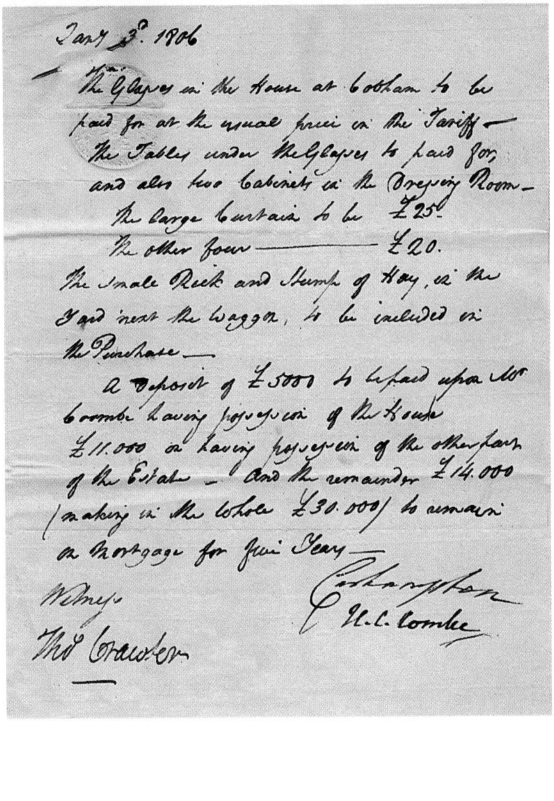

Jan.y 3d. 1806

— The Glasses in the House at Cobham to be
paid for at the usual price in the Tariff —
The Tables under the Glasses to paid for,
and also two Cabinets in the Dressing Room —
The large Curtain to be £25.
The other four ——— £20.
The small Rick and Stump of Hay, in the
Yard next the Waggon, to be included in
the Purchase —
A Deposit of £5000 to be paid upon Mr
Combe having possession of the House
£11.000 on having possession of the other part
of the Estate — And the remainder £14.000
(making in the whole £30.000) to remain
on Mortgage for five Years —

Witness
Thos Crawter

Carhampton
H.C. Combe

37 An extract from the Agreement between Lord Carhampton and Harvey Christian Combe for the purchase of the Cobham estate in 1806. Thomas Crawter, the Cobham land agent, has witnessed the signatures. This part of the Agreement deals with the additional purchase of items of furniture and furnishings together with a hay rick. Combe was to pay £5,000 upon taking possession of the house, and £11,000 upon taking possession of the rest of the estate. The balance of £14,000 was to remain outstanding on mortgage for five years.

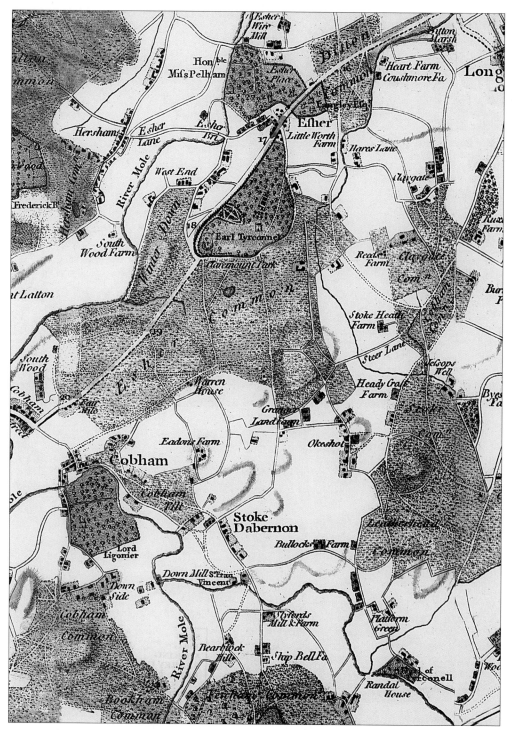

38 This extract from John Cary's map of *c*.1780 shows both Cobham Park and Esher Place (at this time owned by the Pelham family) which Harvey Combe had originally considered purchasing from the Spicer family. It is clear from this map that the Cobham estate provided more scope for expansion than that at Esher.

39 Harvey Christian Combe from the portrait by Benjamin Burnell.

40 This caricature of Harvey Combe as a prize fighter relates to his election fight with William Lushington for the City of London in Parliament in 1789.

41 'The Triumph of Quassia' by James Gillray. Quassia was a drug obtained from the Quassia tree, which is supposed to have supplanted hops in brewing. In 1806 a tax increase was proposed which would have had a damaging effect on smaller brewers but which would have been to the advantage of the larger brewers like Combe.

42 'Hospitality Kicking Avarice Out Of Doors: or New Tenants At A Mansion House.' This satire was published to commemorate Harvey Christian Combe being installed as Lord Mayor of London in 1799.

43 'English Patriots Bowing At The Shrine Of Despotism' by Gillray. This picture satirises the visit made to Napoleon in Paris in 1802 by Combe, Lord Erskine and Charles James Fox. Combe wears his mayoral chain; from his pocket projects 'Essay on Porter Brewing'.

44 The imposing Combe family mausoleum in the churchyard of St Andrew's, Cobham. This photograph shows the mausoleum prior to the removal of the railings for scrap during The Second World War.

45 The agricultural improver John Southey, 15th Lord Somerville, was Harvey Combe's 'neighbour' at Fairmile Farm and helped Combe establish a flock of sheep at Cobham Park.

46 Cobham Park, the main front, from a watercolour by John Hassell dated 1821.

47 Cobham Park, the garden front, from a watercolour by Edward Hassell, *c.*1827.

48 (below) Cobham Park, plan of basement, 1844.

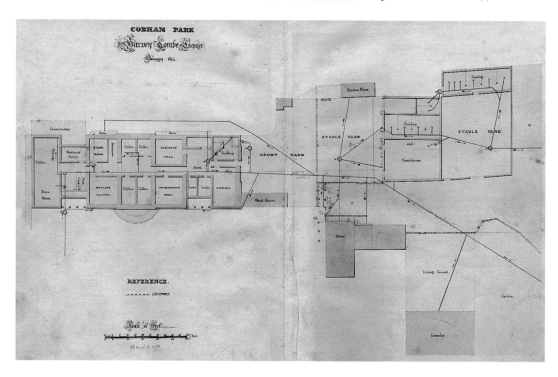

49 Cobham Park mansion across the park, from a watercolour of 1859.

50 The lake and park at Cobham Park, from a watercolour of 1842.

51 The lake and park at Cobham Park, from a watercolour of 1843.

52   Cobham Park, the east end showing the 'gothick' conservatory façade which was probably designed by J.B. Papworth for Lord Carhampton.

53 (above right)   Charlotte Delafield, daughter of Harvey Christian Combe, from a painting by H.W. Pickersgill in the collection of the New York Genealogical & Bibliographical Society. Charlotte married her cousin Joseph Delafield in 1819.

54   Harvey Combe junior, 1839. 'Young Harvey' is seen here on 'Ferdinand' in his role as Master of the Old Berkeley Hunt, after a painting by Abraham Cooper.

55 'Young Harvey' was a man of his times and looked to invest his money in new and modern enterprises. In 1824 he purchased four shares in the Kensington Canal Company which was created by an Act of Parliament 'for widening, deepening, enlarging and making navigable a certain Creek, from or near Counter's Bridge, on the Road from London to Hammersmith, to the River Thames in the county of Middlesex'. The venture was not a success and was later taken over by the Birmingham, Bristol and Thames Junction Railway.

56 Cobham Park and surroundings from a map of 1839. Nos 210, 219 and 218 are the site of the kitchen gardens and 217 is the *Plough Inn*.

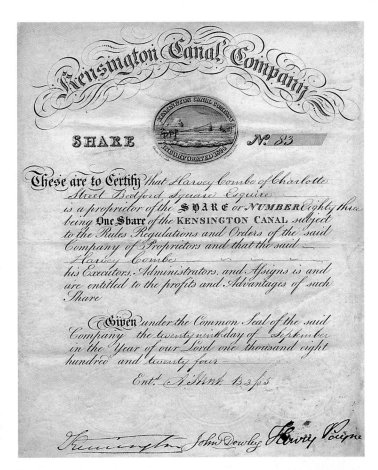

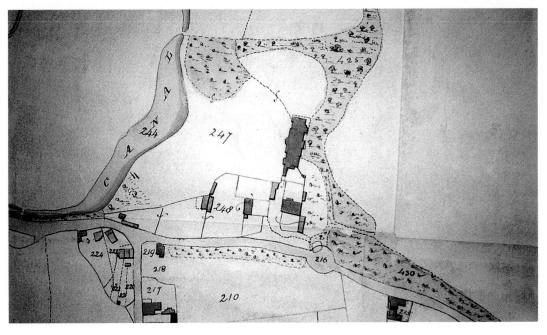

57 Cobham Park mansion across the park, from a water-colour of c.1859.

58 Cobham Park – horse and groom outside the kitchen door of the old mansion.

6

THE COMMANDER-IN-CHIEF

John Louis Ligonier, who purchased the Cobham estate from John Bridges in 1749, was one of the most important military figures of the 18th century. He filled the gap as the nation's hero between the Duke of Marlborough, under whom he had fought at Blenheim in 1704, and the Duke of Wellington. Although a Huguenot of fairly humble origins, Ligonier rose to become Commander-in-Chief of the British Army. In 1720 he received the Colonelcy of the 8th Black Horse, which he made into a crack regiment nicknamed Ligonier's (subsequently the 7th Dragoon Guards). Promoted brigadier-general in 1735, major-general and Governor of Kinsale in 1739, he commanded a division at the beginning of Dettingen-Fontenoy campaign in 1742-7, in which he earned a knighthood and the personal friendship of George II, and ended as commander-on-chief of the British force. During his active service Ligonier took part in no fewer than 23 general actions and 19 sieges without receiving a wound and was held in high regard by all who served under him.

Ligonier was created Lord Ligonier of Enniskillen in 1757, Earl and field-marshal in 1766. He also served as Chief Ranger of Ireland with a residence in Dublin and, when his term of office came to an end, Ligonier found that it was necessary to look to England to provide the opportunity and occasion for the recreations of society and sport that he so much enjoyed. He had already established a London residence at 12 Audley Street but needed a country retreat close to the capital.[1]

Unfortunately little is known of his life at Cobham as whatever of his correspondence survives deals almost exclusively with military matters. However, here and there it is possible to find some mention of life in Surrey, such as a letter to Sir Charles Frederick written from Cobham in April 1755, in which Ligonier says, 'I go on better every hour I stay here and my little farm looks more pleasing every day'.[2] To describe his estate as 'my little farm' seems modest in the extreme. In 1769, when he insured the house with the Hand In Hand Insurance Company, it was described as being 'finished in a Grand Manner.' The insurance policy stated that the house was four storeys high covering a ground area 63 feet by 47 feet. It had two identical wings, each consisting of three parts, one 46 feet by 17 feet 6 inches; the other two measured 16 feet by 13 feet. One wing contained the kitchen and bakehouse, the other a washhouse and other offices. The whole property was insured for £5,000.

Shortly after moving to Cobham, Ligonier held a weekend house party including among his guests the Prime Minister, William Pitt the elder. The party later moved to nearby Claremont, home of the Duke of Newcastle, another of Ligonier's friends. In 1756 the wife of Admiral Boscawen of Hatchlands near Guildford visited Ligonier and described him as 'a charming old man … polite, conversible, easy, free and very cheerful'.[3] One of Ligonier's closest friends over many years was the eccentric Lady Mary Coke, who often stayed for weekends at Cobham. Horace Walpole later described Ligonier as 'Polished for foppery by age, and from living in a more thinking country, he had all the gallant gaiety of his nation and was universally beloved and respected.'

Although Cobham was planned as a place of retreat from his public life, when a French invasion was threatened in 1759, the house became his headquarters while laying out the military camp on Send Heath near Woking. Earlier, following the surrender of Cherbourg in 1758, a number of cannon were captured and dragged in triumph through the streets of London in a victory parade. Ligonier took some of these cannon for the adornment of the gardens at Cobham.

Throughout his time at Cobham Ligonier sought every opportunity to enlarge his estate by purchasing adjoining land holdings. In 1750 he acquired three acres of meadow or pasture from Henry Weston and three years later he purchased an estate known as 'Fragges' together with 21 acres of land from Anne Toye and her son Richard.[4] In 1758 Ligonier purchased a 'Capital Messuage and divers lands adjoining' from Elizabeth Martin. The house was described as being in Poulters Lane which was the old name for the Downside Road. This property almost certainly stood on the site of what is now called Cossins Farm, adjoining the former 'Botells', and was probably once owned by the Sutton family.[5] This last purchase included lands within the old open field known as Down Field and would have made a very useful and sizeable addition to the estate extending in a southerly direction.

In February 1759 Ligonier made his most important addition to the estate when he purchased Downe Hall from The Hon. George Fox Lane for £4,000.[6] Downe Hall, also known as Downe Place, had been the most important estate in Cobham in medieval times and was a 'reputed manor'. It lay to the south of Cobham Park and was separated from it by Downe Field. The history of this property can be traced back to Edward I when William de la Dune, Keeper of the King's Hanaper, lived there.[7] The King appears to have made several visits to the house when he was passing through Surrey. In the 17th century Downe Hall was owned by John Downe who left the property to his nephew George Smyther. In 1720 the Smyther family sold Downe Hall to Frances, Viscountess Lanesborough who had earlier purchased the manor of Cobham from the Gavell family. When she died, Lady Lanesborough left Downe Hall to her grandsons of the Fox family and it was George Lane Fox who sold to Ligonier. It was probably about this time that the confusion arose concerning the original location of Downe Hall.

Manning and Bray's *History of Surrey*, published in 1809, refers to John Bridges' house as replacing Downe Hall and this tradition was carried on until recent times.

It is only during the last few years that research has clarified the situation and shown that Downe Hall was on the site of the present Down Farm and Cobham Park mansion on the site of Bridge House Farm. It seems likely that after 1759 Ligonier and his successors began to refer to their house as Downe Place.

It is not clear who built the house which now stands at Down Farm. It has been dated to the early part of the 18th century by the Domestic Buildings Research Group (Surrey). Two excavations undertaken by the Surrey Archaeological Society in 2004 have produced evidence of much earlier occupation of the site, possibly dating back to Anglo-Saxon times.[8] A large curved pond which partly surrounds the house could be the remains of a medieval moat. It was not uncommon in the medieval period to construct such a feature which would have been used as a show of status rather than for defensive purposes. Perhaps William de la Dune had the moat dug to impress the King on one of his visits.

By acquiring Downe Place Ligonier began to push the southern boundary of his estate as far as the parish boundary between Cobham and Bookham. Ligonier added a further 40 acres to the estate when in 1764 he acquired a copyhold property which had once belonged to the Porter family.[9] In 1768 Ligonier purchased a 'Messuage and Land … formerly Goodyers' which comprised lands between 'Poulters Lane' (now Downside Road) and Downe Field as well as land on the opposite side of the road in Westcrofte and 'Baggs Mead' which was five acres to the south of the river Mole in what is now known as Plough Meadows.[10] Ligonier's final acquisition was a three-acre copyhold estate at Downside called 'Heathornes' which he purchased in 1769.[11] This piecemeal acquisition of land by Ligonier brought with it various complications including rights of way which he needed to extinguish or divert if he were to maintain security and privacy. In 1765 he entered into an Agreement with a representative group of Cobham inhabitants to enclose one footpath which crossed his estate.[12]

According to the Memoirs of the Reverend Dr John Trusler (see page 34), the Field Marshal 'residing at Cobham was ever disposed to be of use to the parish & being commander in chief had this village to be struck off the Record book in the War office, so that no soldiers were ever quartered there & this book not having been inspected for many years the Indulgence was continued for a long time after his death. This & his beneficence of all occasions led the people to think, it was only to ask and have; thus convinced of his Lord's friendly disposition to the parish, & the Church having but five bells (which for want of solidity tinkled as it cracked) & room for a sixth, it was determined by a half reasoning vestry to solicit his Lordship to present them with another, to render them as they said more tuneable. On this application Lord Ligonier expressed his readiness at all times to gratify the parish & asked the Churchwardens, who were the applicants what a sixth bell would cost. Not more said they than £50. "Well then", returned he, "to convince you of my good will I will give the parish 200£" – (Here he paused and the bell-committee were in rapture) 'if you will remove four of the present five. One bell is sufficient for calling the people to Church & more than one in a Country village is not only a nuisance

to everyone within their sound, but is an encouragement to idol people, singers &
other to waster their time which might be better employed".'

Although he never married, Ligonier was a great ladies' man and enjoyed a
lifelong reputation for his fondness for the opposite sex. He fathered a child named
Penelope by Penelope Miller of Horsleydown in London whom he fully acknowledged
and supported. At Cobham Ligonier is reputed to have kept a small harem of
young women and the scandalous publication *Chrysal*, in 1762, printed the story
of his seduction of a local milkmaid called Hebe Watson. Ligonier, walking in his
garden at Cobham, saw her carrying a pail of milk and was so delighted by her
comeliness that he gave her half a crown. This she passed to her mother who, seeing
her daughter as a steady source of income, arranged for the General's valet to make
a business deal. Ligonier also had affairs with several leading actresses of his day,
including Kitty Fisher, and 'at Covent Garden Mrs Woff-n (Peg Woffington) used
to sup with Ligonier in the Green Room on mutton pies. In return for her favours
the General presented her with a pair of diamond show buckles.'

Lord Ligonier died in 1770 aged 89 and was buried in an unmarked grave in
St Andrew's church, Cobham.[13] As he had never married he had no legitimate heir.
In his will, the field marshal provided that his nephew Edward should have a life
interest in the estate and so opened another chapter in its history.

7

SCANDAL AND DIVORCE

It was during the incumbency of the next occupants of Cobham Park that the house was to become the scene of one of the most colourful chapters in its history. Edward Ligonier, the field marshal's nephew, was the illegitimate son of Francis Ligonier and Anne Freeman. Francis Ligonier had led a distinguished military career and died after leaving his sickbed to rally his troops at the battle of Falkirk Muir in 1746.[1] After his father's death Edward, or 'Ned' as the family called him, was given over to be raised by his uncle who oversaw his education and military career. It was no doubt through his uncle that, in 1763, Edward was appointed aide-de-camp to George III. According to some sources it was also through his uncle that Edward met and married Penelope, the 16-year-old daughter of George Pitt, Earl Rivers of Stratfield Saye in Hampshire. The couple were married on 16 December 1766 in the English Ambassador's chapel in Paris. Although the wedding was a quiet affair, the marriage was to become a *cause célèbre*, resulting in one of the most famous divorce trials of the 18th century.

When his uncle died Edward succeeded to the Irish viscountcy and a life tenancy of the Cobham estate. Lord Rivers celebrated this event by commissioning Gainsborough to paint two life-sized portraits of his daughter and son-in-law, to commemorate the event. When, in 1771, the paintings were exhibited at the Royal Academy, Gainsborough was censured by the critics for having painted Edward's horse as prominently as the Viscount himself. Penelope is depicted holding drawing pencils and surrounded by other elements suggesting that she was an educated and an artistic women. Ironically the public exhibition of these portraits coincided with the discovery of Penelope's adulterous affairs and one of the most colourful chapters in Cobham Park's history.

The scandal caused by Penelope's extra-marital affairs would perhaps today pass largely unnoticed. However, at the time it became the talk of the town and the published account of the resultant divorce trial, together with other contemporary literature, provides an almost hour-by-hour account of her amorous escapades played out against the backdrop of the Ligoniers' London and Cobham residences.

The matter first came to the public attention after a duel fought in Green Park in May 1771. *The Public Advertiser* published the following report:

> Last Tuesday Night was fought in the Green Park, between Lord V—t L—and Comte A---I, a Piedmonte Nobleman, in which the latter was wounded. The

Detection of a Criminal Amour was the unhappy Occasion of this Affair. Nothing could be more determined, than the cool and resolute Conduct of the injured Husband on this unfortunate Occasion, of such a Nature, that legal Redress must be the Consequence.

The 'injured Husband' was Edward Ligonier and his antagonist was the Italian poet and playwright Count Vittorio Alfieri. Alfieri was from the Italian town of Asti, famous to this day for its sparkling wine. He was a talented, flamboyant, good-looking man with red hair, always heavily perfumed. He also had a strong reputation as a ladies' man. Alfieri had first set eyes on Penelope during an earlier visit to London. On his return to England in 1770 he decided to seek out the lady who had captured his heart. Unable to visit her London house, Alfieri took the opportunity to see her from a distance, first at the opera and then in Hyde Park. As spring approached Alfieri learned that Penelope was to return to Cobham for some seven or eight months. Unable to bear the thought of being so long separated, he boldly called at the London house when the Earl was away thereby, in his words, 'inflaming even more' the passion which he felt for her.

In May 1770 Lord and Lady Ligonier left London for Cobham and on hearing that the Earl would be in London for a few days, Alfieri boldly decided to make a visit to Cobham for a secret assignation with Penelope. He later recounted in his memoirs, 'It was already dark and I pursued my way on foot to a little door in the park wall where I found her awaiting my arrival. I entered the house, fully persuaded that no one had seen me. These assignations, instead of satisfying, only augmented our passion, for the dread of separation was ever present in our minds.'

A few days later, after Alfieri had returned to London, he had a bad fall from his horse whilst trying to jump a high gate. This resulted in a dislocated arm and his surgeon ordered him to bed. Alfieri wrote, 'Those alone who have felt the dominion of a passion as ardent as mine can form an idea of my rage when I found myself confined to bed on the evening of the happy day which was fixed for our second assignation.' Eventually passion overcame pain and Alfieri set out again for Cobham 'to the house of my mistress in a carriage with a postillion, I decided to leave it in good time. With this view I quitted it about two miles distance from the place of my destination and pursued the remainder of the way on foot.' After crossing the churchyard, Alfieri soon arrived at the park but finding his usual entrance door shut he was forced to climb over the fence. 'I did not leave till day-break and departed in the same manner as I entered.'

This visit was later recalled at the divorce trial by the postillion, Thomas Johnson, who had travelled with Alfieri from Kingston and put him down in Cobham, a short distance from the *Ship Inn*, later renamed the *Tartar*. Although Alfieri was 'much disguised in his dress, having on an old blue great coat, with a round post boy's hat and one of his arms bound up in a black crape cling', Johnson recognised the Count's red hair and noticed that under his great coat 'he had a very handsome coat, and was particularly smart about his legs and feet, having clean white silk stockings, and neat shoes and buckles on'. Alfieri told the boy to wait for him and then set off on foot for Cobham Park. Alfieri crossed a stile by the *Tartar* and followed a footpath that can still be traced in parts across the former Tartar Fields and down into Hogshill Lane and Cobham village. He returned to the *Tartar* in the early hours of the next morning and was taken back to Kingston.

By chance it happened that it was the same postillion who drove Ligonier back to Cobham the following day and it was he who told him of the Count's nocturnal visit. On arriving home, Ligonier's servants corroborated the post boy's story. William Pepper, Nathaniel Sandy and William Fletcher[2] were all employed by Ligonier on the Cobham estate. Pepper reported that he had seen Alfieri in the fields near the house on that Sunday evening and, suspecting that he was heading to Cobham Park, had immediately returned to the house and shut and bolted all windows and doors. Later that evening Pepper and Sandy suspected that Alfieri was somewhere on the premises and toured the house checking the windows and doors. They discovered that a bar across the garden entrance had been lifted and that the window was partly open. They promptly secured the window again and went to bed.

The following morning, Pepper, Sandy and Fletcher went into the state bedroom and found 'that the carpet at the bottom of the bed was much rumpled, and there were then two large dints at the bottom of the bed, as if two persons had been sitting on it, and the bed in the middle appeared as if somebody had been laying on it, and a little above the middle of the bed, was a round place, about the size of a person's head covered with powder.' Penelope Ligonier later confessed to her maid servant that it was she who had arranged Alfieri's clandestine visit and had admitted him to the house and hidden him in 'the Red Room'.

Upon hearing his servants' reports, Ligonier became convinced of his wife's unfaithfulness and faced her with accusations and witnesses, declaring that he no longer considered her to be his wife and that he would sue for divorce. Penelope immediately dispatched a trusted messenger to Alfieri informing him of what had happened. 'The courier, who was lavishly rewarded, nearly destroyed a horse in riding post-haste to London where he arrived in less than two hours, an hour before the husband.' But Alfieri was not at home and so he missed both the courier and the enraged husband. Alfieri later wrote, 'it was fortunate for me on this occasion that I had dislocated the left arm and not the right and that I did not receive the letter of my mistress till after our recontre, as I might not have conducted myself so well.'

A few days later Ligonier eventually confronted Alfieri at the Opera House in Haymarket. What happened was fully reported in a contemporary newspaper.

> The L—d L—r having lately discovered that too great a intimacy subsisted between his lady and Count A—I, went to his country seat, where she then was, and after expressing his displeasure at her behaviour, sent her directly to her father Mr G—e P—t, to whom he declared that he would have her no longer, and that at the next session of Parliament he intended to sue for divorce. He then went afterwards in search of Count A—I, whom he found at the Opera house, in the Spanish Ambassador's box, and sent him word to step outside for a moment; he then let him know that he was thoroughly acquainted with everything that had passed between his wife and him, and the determination he had taken in

consequence thereof; and that he insisted upon having satisfaction for the injury he had received from him; to which Count A—I answering, that he was pleased, not withstanding he had still his arm in a sling, on account of his clavicular having been put out of joint by a fall two days before; they went into St James's Park where a duel ensued: but after fighting for a short time, L---d L—r thinking his antagonist was wounded, told him that he was satisfied in having done what became a man of honour to do that he would trouble him no more.

Alfieri's account, written in his memoirs some years later, adds a little more romance and dash to the story. 'My heart was agitated', Alfieri writes, 'with a thousand different passions, I thought I heard my name pronounced in a high tone by some one at the door of the box. By a kind of mechanical impulse I opened the box door and immediately went out … The first person I saw was the husband of my mistress.'

Nathaniel Sandy later stated that Ligonier had gone from his London house to Bond Street, where he borrowed a sword from a sword cutler. Thomas Byrne, a box-keeper at the Opera House, recalled how Ligonier had arrived at the theatre wearing his boots and 'was quite in an undress'. Ligonier asked Alfieri to go with him to Green Park. The following is Alfieri's romantic version of what then happened.

> It was about half past seven in the evening. During the long days of the summer the Opera begins at six o'clock. From the Haymarket we took the road to St James's Park; thence we adjourned to a large field termed Green Park where, having sought a retired corner, we drew our swords. In proceeding along Pall Mall he spoke several times, reproaching me with having clandestinely entered his house on various occasions, and demanded from me the reason for my conduct. Though I felt the upbraiding of my conscience and was sensible of his just ground of resentment against me, notwithstanding my distraction at the time, I yet preserved sufficient presence of mind not to make any other reply than to affirm that the charge was not true; but that if he gave any credit to it I was ready to give him satisfaction.

Ligonier then told Alfieri that his wife had 'avowed all to me herself'. At this Alfieri was forced to admit his part in the affair – an admission he immediately regretted. On arriving in Green Park, Ligonier noticed that Alfieri's arm was in a sling and generously offered not to fight. The Count declined and put himself on guard. Alfieri continued, 'I was never proficient in the use of the sword. I rushed on him contrary to all the rules of art, like a madman as I was, for in fact, I wished to meet death at his hands.' The duel continued for some minutes with Alfieri always on the attack and Ligonier on the defensive. However, at last Ligonier wounded his opponent between the elbow and the wrist. He then lowered his sword and said that he was satisfied. Later, when Alfieri's wound was being treated, he examined his own sword and dramatically recorded that he 'found the blade notched like a saw and diminished nearly two thirds, so furiously had I attacked my adversary'. Ligonier's conduct towards his wife's lover was considered to be most generous and gentlemanly and resulted in a satirical publication that appeared a few days later entitled:

The GENEROUS HUSBAND; or the HISTORY of Lord LAELIUS
and the fair EMILIA. Containing likewise the Genuine
Memoirs of ASMODEI, the presented Piedmonteze Count,
from the Time of Birth to his late ignominious Fall in Hyde Park.

Considering his wound 'but a mere scratch', Alfieri returned to the theatre, where he stayed for a quarter of an hour before deciding to visit the house of Lady Ligonier's sister. 'On entering the apartment, the first object which presented itself to my view was my mistress herself. This unexpected meeting agitated me greatly and I nearly fainted.' Lady Ligonier then recounted to Alfieri 'some details respecting this unfortunate affair, which were not however perfectly accurate. It was reserved for me to learn the truth through another channel.'

Lady Ligonier said that her husband had learned of Alfieri's first visit to Cobham and of how the Count had left his horse and walked to the park. It seems that her husband had employed one of his servants at Cobham to spy on her in his absence. This he did and he observed Alfieri's second visit to Cobham. Added to this was the unfortunate coincidence of Alfieri and Ligonier using the same postillion.

The following day an emboldened Alfieri went again to visit Lady Ligonier and spent the day with her. 'She wept without ceasing, protesting every moment that she loved me beyond expression. She assured me that the scandal of this affair and the dishonour with which she was loaded, would be amply compensated by the happiness of living always with me; but she added that she was certain I would never marry her.' Much to Alfieri's chagrin, during a further visit to Penelope made later that week, she admitted to a previous affair with a groom in her husband's service at Cobham. It was this very groom who had been employed to spy on Lady Ligonier. After hearing of the duel the groom had made a full confession to Lord Ligonier of a relationship which he claimed had lasted three years. The jealous groom urged his master not to give way to despair but rather to consider 'the loss of such a woman as a blessing than a curse'.

Alfieri could hardly believe what he was hearing and after 'cursing, groaning, crying aloud. Distraught with anger and pain yet still madly in love with this unworthy creature', he left her saying that he would never marry her 'that if chance had after our union unveiled to me such infamous conduct I would have killed her with my own hand; and that I should have destroyed myself at the same time.'

Despite all this Alfieri promised Penelope that he would always be her friend and never abandon her. However the final ignominy came the following morning when Alfieri picked up a newspaper and 'glancing casually at the first thing I saw was my own name. I … found that it not only gave a very full and accurate account of my own adventure but even the name and particulars of the groom my rival, together with the ample confession he had made to his master.' Alfieri's real punishment came when, reading this account, he realised that Penelope had only confessed to him after she had spoken with the newspaper and realised that she would be found out anyway. Alfieri was furious and 'flew to her house and, after loading her with the most abusive and contemptuous epithets, intermingled with expressions of the most ardent love, tenderness, and sorrow, I departed vowing that I would never see her more, though in less than an hour I was so desperately weak as to return and I spent the whole day with her.'

Eventually, Penelope Ligonier decided to leave England for the unlikely retreat of a French convent. Alfieri accompanied her and her sister-in-law to Rochester and then returned to London. On his return he discovered that he was being made the principal party of the divorce proceedings on account of her adultery and that he was to be sued for £20,000 damages. Alfieri promptly left England for The Hague nursing a wound that was 'very deep'. On 10 December 1772 Lord Ligonier was granted a divorce and later married the daughter of the Lord Chancellor. Thirteen years after the divorce Penelope was reported as having married Captain Smith, 'a trooper in the blues' at Northampton.

Penelope Ligonier's reputation was such that a contemporary satire by William Combe, entitled 'The Diablo-Lady', included her among the five claimants for the queenship of Hell. In an engraving accompanying the satire Penelope is shown in riding dress holding a paper headed 'The Countess and the Stable Boy'. Another contemporary writer claimed that she was a 'classic example of depravity'. Penelope was depicted in other cruel caricatures of the period, one of which related directly to her affair with the groom and was entitled 'The Stable Adventure, or the Lucky Expedient'. Alfieri later had a passionate affair with Princess Louis de Stolbey who, in 1772, had married the Young Pretender, Charles Edward Stuart. Alfieri never forgot Penelope and was deeply moved when, some twenty years later, he met her when he was boarding a ship at Dover. He wrote, 'She appeared scarcely less lovely than twenty years before when I had parted from her.'

The Reverend Dr John Trusler who lived on part of the Cobham Park estate in the 1770s (see Chapter Eight) wrote his own account of Lady Ligonier's affairs in the second and unpublished part of his Memoirs.[3] Of Lady Ligonier's friendship with Lord Tankerville's sister, Lady Frances Bennet, Trusler wrote, 'These ladies were too often together for their own good … they were both seen in Lord Ligonier's stables romping with the grooms.' He had been at school with Edward Ligonier and was well acquainted both with him and his uncle. Edward appointed Trusler to be his Chaplain.

Trusler recorded a particular episode at Cobham Park when the Field Marshall held a ball for his servants and 'bad them invite the farmers and shopkeepers daughters & their sweethearts in the neighbourhood. The Gentlemen also at such times always partook of the merriment & danced with them.' Penelope Ligonier, bedecked with diamonds, chose to dance with a 'black servant of Lord Tyrconnel'. Seeing her dance with this servant, Tyrconnel's coachman, who had drunk too much punch, was heard to say loud enough for her to hear that he would 'consent to go to hell hereafter if he could but have one nights lodging with that woman'. Penelope Ligonier was advised to leave the room but the coachman ran after, caught her, pressed her to the wall and kissed her. It seems that Penelope may have offered him some encouragement and it was after this episode that Edward became suspicious of her.

Of Penelope, Trusler wrote that 'though a very fine figure & a delicate looking woman' she was 'was tall, muscular & masculine in her manners, she disliked the company of women, never drank tea and was fond of beer & meat for breakfast'. She would often swig beer from a bottle and was 'more powerful in her arms than most men'. She kept a stable and a dogkennel and 'took pleasure in shooting, hunting, driving & rowing'. She would drive 'a low phaeton with a pair of high mettled horses … at full speed over low banks and ploughed lands.' However, she also displayed femine accomplishments such as speaking French, and she 'danced & sung well, played well on the piano & harp, drew like an artist & was a fine embroideress.'

Not long after his very public humiliation, Edward Ligonier was made to consider significant events of a totally different nature that took place both locally and across the nation which would change the appearance of the landscape for ever. By the 18th century the large open fields of the parish which had functioned well during the medieval period were deemed unsuitable for modern farming practice. In addition the wars with France were putting pressure on the country to produce as much home-grown food as possible. Some enclosure of the open fields had taken place by agreement over the preceding centuries but this had been largely piecemeal. In 1779 Ligonier together with Thomas Page of Pointers, lord of the manor of Cobham, and other leading landowners applied to Parliament for a private Act called 'An Act for Dividing and Inclosing the Common and Open fields within the Parish of Cobham, in the County of Surrey.'4

One of the largest open fields was Down Field which had in 1598 comprised some 152 acres. This field lay to the south of Cobham Park and separated it from Down Place which had been purchased by Field Marshal Ligonier in 1759. Ligonier and his trustees held strips in the common field and were therefore entitled to an allocation under the award which followed the passing of the Act. It was particularly in their interest to acquire as much as possible of the former Down Field so that the estate could be made more secure, compact and manageable. Ligonier was allotted a total of approximately 34 acres. The largest area which he acquired was 'a field called the Ore'. This comprised some 19 acres and lay to the south of the road which led through to Downside Mill. Other lands allotted to Ligonier were in the Upper and Lower Marsh which lay just to the west of the river Mole in the area which is now crossed by the bridle way leading from Downside to Ash Ford on Cobham Tilt. Further significant changes in the appearance of Cobham that would affect the estate were to take place when the commons and wastes were enclosed following another Act of Parliament passed in 1793.

Edward Ligonier died in 1782 and was buried in St Andrew's church, Cobham. The house remained in the hands of his uncle's executors.

8

TO LET

Edward Ligonier's occupancy of the Cobham estate had been as a life tenant under the terms of his uncle's will and after his death it was left to the lawyers to sort out who was then entitled to the residuary estate. This proved to be a lengthy task and from 1782 to 1801, whilst the legal settlement was being resolved and a purchaser found the property was let for short periods to a variety of tenants. Unfortunately there is nothing in the estate papers relating to these short-term lettings and it is necessary to look elsewhere to find who might have been living at the property. The best sources for that purpose are the returns for Land Tax.

The Cobham Land Tax returns run from 1780 to the 1830s and provide the names of property owners and their tenants.[1] Francis Lloyd, one of Ligonier's trustees, is recorded as the proprietor of Ligonier's estate for 1783 to 1788. After that it is shown under the names of Lloyd and his fellow trustees until the sale of the estate to Lord Carhampton in 1801. In 1783 and 1784 the occupier is given as Francis Lloyd himself although it is doubtful whether he actually lived there. From 1785 to 1787 the tenant was Thomas Parry.[2] The property is then shown as being empty for several years until 1793. However, it is clear from other sources that the property was let for short periods during this time and one of the tenants was the Shakespearean scholar Edmond Malone (1741-1812).

Born in Dublin, Edmond Malone practised in Ireland as a lawyer and journalist before moving to London in 1777. There he numbered among his literary friends Samuel Johnson and Horace Walpole. He was also an associate of the statesmen Edmund Burke and George Canning and a friend of Sir Joshua Reynolds, who painted his portrait in 1778. Malone is now best remembered for his research into the works of Shakespeare. He was the first great Shakespearean collector and editor. In 1778 he wrote *An Attempt to Ascertain the Order in Which the Plays of Shakespeare Were Written*. Malone's *Historical Account of the Rise and Progress of the English Stage, and of the Economy and Usages of the Ancient Theatres in England*, published in 1800, was the first treatise on English drama based on original sources. His own edition of Shakespeare in 11 volumes appeared in 1790. A new edition, unfinished at his death, was completed by James Boswell, the son of Samuel Johnson's biographer. This work became the standard edition of Shakespeare's writing for more than a century.

Malone came to Cobham for a short spell during the summer of 1788. He moved there with his sisters and his brother's wife, Lady Sunderlin, whilst his own home was being redecorated. Malone loved his interlude in rural Surrey and wrote of a 'summer in a fine country and a very pleasant retirement, though within 20 miles of London'. At Cobham Malone was visited by his friends John Courtney[3] and Robert Jephson.[4] In September 1788 Courtney wrote to James Boswell senior: 'You would be delighted with the Aristocratic dignity and Convenience of this Mansion; especially with the Addition of Malone's Hospitality.'[5] James Boswell responded to his friend's invitation to join the party at Cobham and spent a day and a half there the following month.

Returning to the Land Tax, the next recorded occupier is Sir Henry Sheridan who was at the house in 1793. Little is known of Sir Henry save that he lived at Havering Hall, Essex in 1802 and, before that, at Elfords House, Hawkhurst, Kent. In 1794 the occupier is shown as Lady Robert Manners (1737-1829). Mary Manners was the widow of Lord Robert Manners, third son of the Marquis of Granby[6] and grandson of the 3rd Duke of Rutland. Lord Robert Manners had been a captain in the navy and died as a result of fighting the French in the West Indies in 1782 in the Battle of the Saints. Manners was captain of *Resolution* under the command of Sir George Rodney. In the action Manners received several severe wounds, in addition to having one leg shot off. Despite this it was hoped that he would recover. However, lockjaw set in and he died on the return trip to England. He was described in his day as a young man of great gallantry and promise and was 'universally regretted by the nation as well as the navy'.

Other names associated with Cobham Park during this period are those of Alexander Raby the ironmaster, the Reverend Dr John Trusler, and a 'Mrs Wedgwood'.

Alexander Raby came from a family of Wealden ironmasters. In 1770 he purchased Downside Mill. The former corn mill had been used for the production of paper in the late 17th and early 18th centuries. Raby converted it to provide power for the production of iron goods. What had formerly been a rural area suddenly became the site of heavy industrial use and the effect on the neighbourhood must have been considerable. Another of Raby's enterprises at Coxes Lock near Weybridge saw the installation of a 'great hammer' nicknamed 'Hackering Jack' which delivered some 2,700 blows an hour. The noise was so great that local landowners and residents objected. We are left to guess at what the residents of Cobham made of the Downside enterprise. When Raby left the area in about 1805 he moved to Llanelli in South Wales where he was able to make good use of the natural resources of the area and develop what had been a small fishing village into the major industrial centre it became in the 19th century. At Cobham Raby leased some of the Cobham Park lands and built himself a substantial house close to the mill. Land Tax records appear to indicate that Raby actually resided in Cobham Park mansion for a short period – probably while his own house was being built. After Raby left Cobham his house was demolished and its site reverted to farm land.[7]

The Reverend Doctor John Trusler was an entrepreneur of a different sort. The son of the proprietor of the public tea gardens in Marylebone, Trusler became a priest in 1759. He pursued a number of innovative ways in which to earn money, one of which was the printing in imitation handwriting of a collection of sermons which he sold for a shilling each in order to save clergy both study and the trouble of transcription. The bishops frowned upon this publication and discouraged its use. Trusler employed various artists to illustrate his publications including Thomas Bewick and William Blake. Trusler was not happy with Blake's work and heavily criticised it, accusing Blake of 'obscurity and incompetence'. One of Trusler's more successful publications was his *Practical Husbandry, or the Art of Farming with certainty of gain* which was first published in 1780. This contains a number of references to farming in the Cobham area. Trusler moved to Cobham in 1769 and lived for a while at the house now called Ham Manor, close to Cobham Mill. According to the second part of his unpublished Memoirs, Trusler soon became 'very intimate in the family of Field Marshall [*sic*] John Earl Ligonier'.[8] Trusler had been at school with the Field Marshal's nephew and later became Edward's chaplain. Trusler moved to live in a cottage on the Cobham Park estate and from there he wrote his book on farming.[9] In his Memoirs Trusler records, 'One of my chief amusements in the country was improving & decorating the grounds about my cottage at Cobham. I possessed one acre of garden ground but had so contrived it as by concealing the boundary, by plantations beyond it & sunk fences, to make the surrounding country my own and strangers in walking round it have fancied it to extend to miles.' Whilst living in Cobham, Trusler witnessed the dramatic changes to the local landscape brought about by the enclosure of the old open fields in 1779 followed by the even more dramatic changes brought about by the enclosure of the commons and wastes which followed another Act of Parliament in 1793.[10] Downside Common, which was stated to comprise about 380 acres, lay to the south of Cobham Park and stretched from the present hamlet of Downside to the boundary of Cobham parish with the parishes of Great Bookham, Effingham, and Ockham.

The trustees of Ligonier's estate were particularly concerned by a possible reduction in its value if valuable grazing on the adjoining Downside Common were lost. A document in the Surrey History Centre sets out the following 'Objections to the proposed Inclosure of Downside Common & Chatley Heath in the Parish of Cobham':

> The Ligonier Estate which was rated to the Land Tax in 1787 at £540 and now at £473 the house being unlet, lies in the most convenient situation for the commoning upon Downside (the most valuable waste in the Manor) and as by the present Bill the whole of this common will be inclosed the annual value of this estate will be reduced upwards of £40 a year – Whereas Estates situated on the north side of the River will not suffer any diminution of annual value as they will retain as convenient and valuable rights of common as they now enjoy – and yet they will receive an equal advantage by being enfranchised and discharged from Heriots.

It has been hinted that this estate is so situated that it may conveniently common of other wastes and particularly if a Sheep Bridge was erected across the River to the Tilt. The occupiers of this Estate have scarcely ever thought it worth their attention to send cattle or sheep to any of the other commons and if this Bridge was to be erected, it is not imagined that they would make great use of it as the Tilt Common is already greatly overstocked from its contiguity to the Town of Cobham, added to the inconvenience of driving the sheep across to an extreme point of the farms – Whereas at present every field adjoins Downside – and as to the cows the whole of that beneficial commonage would be intirely lost from the distance and inconvenience of the ford.

A sheep bridge was not built and it was not until a century later that the Cobham Park estate acquired any land on the north side of the river.[11]

The last recorded tenant of Cobham Park is shown on the Land Tax as 'Mrs Wedgwood'. It is not clear which Mrs Wedgwood this was but she is likely to have been either the widow of Josiah Wedgwood I, the great potter, or the wife of his son, also called Josiah. Josiah Wedgwood II and his family lived at Stoke D'Abernon Manor House between 1795 and 1800 where they entertained the poet Coleridge.

Eventually the lawyers concluded their work on dealing with the ownership of Cobham Park and, in the opening year of the 19th century, the estate passed to a new owner.

9

'ONE OF THE MOST UNPOPULAR MEN IN ENGLAND'

The ingredients of Irish connections, military matters and sexual scandal, which were heavily mixed into Cobham Park during the time of the Ligoniers, were to be found again in the next owner. In 1801 the estate was purchased from the Ligonier trustees by Henry Lawes Luttrell, 2nd Earl of Carhampton (1743-1821), and eldest son of Simon Luttrell, 1st Earl, by his wife Maria, the daughter and heiress of Sir Nicholas Lawes, Governor of Jamaica.

The Luttrells were an old Irish family who could trace their descent back to Sir Geoffrey Luttrell in the time of King John. Their home, Luttrellstown, became one of the chief castles in the County of Dublin. Another branch of the family settled at Dunster Castle in Somerset. Over the centuries the Luttrells' name acquired notoriety for their harsh dealings. Colonel Henry Luttrell was assassinated in 1717 and from this time it is said that 'a cloud of evil tradition and unpopularity' hung over the family. The hatred felt towards them in Ireland is shown in legends that surround a place at Luttrellstown called Devil's Mill. A local story said that this commemorated a mill erected by satanic agency for Colonel Henry Luttrell, who invoked the aid of Satan, but by outwitting him was successful in escaping with his life.

Henry Luttrell's son Simon was created Baron Irnham and Earl of Carhampton, titles that he took from property belonging to the English Luttrells. Simon Luttrell left Ireland and made his principal residence in England. Like his father, Simon Luttrell had a rather unsavoury reputation and was considered in his day to be 'the biggest reprobate in England'. By strange coincidence it was he who was satirised as Satan in the cartoon based on William Combe's satirical poem The Diabolady that depicted Lady Ligonier as one of the contenders for his hand as the Queen of Hell (see plate 24). In an earlier poem called The Diaboliad Lord Irnham is summoned before the Devil as one having a strong claim to succeed him as King of Hell. The poem concludes:

> But as he spoke there issued from the crowd
> Irnham the base, the cruel, and the proud
> And eager cried, 'I boast superior claim
> To Hell's dark throne – and Irnham is my name'

It seems to have been a matter of 'like father – like son' when it came to the Luttrells. Henry and his father had fierce tempers and quarrelled perpetually. There is a story that, when once challenged to a duel by his father, Henry refused the summons because 'it was not given by a gentleman'. Henry's father once told him 'I can forgive you a thousand youthful follies, I know what it was to be young myself, and I should think you no son of mine, if the women entirely escaped your notice; but remember, of all the foolish things you do, let marriage be the last.'[1] Following this advice Henry is said to have 'romped through a multitude of complying beauties', one of whom was Arabella Bolton whose posthumous memoirs were published in 1770.

It seems that Arabella, a gardener's daughter living near Woodstock, was seduced by young Henry whilst an undergraduate at Oxford. The story is also referred to in an 'Ode to Colonel L ----' in the *New Foundling Hospital for Wit*. According to Miss Bolton's memoirs, the young Henry, when studying at Oxford, stayed with friends of his father in a house in which she was employed. Having fallen for her charms he set about administering to her 'the most powerful opiate' in a glass of wine. He then carried her to the housekeeper's bedroom and 'there perpetrated such an act of barbarity and villainy, as must shock not only the virtuous, but even the most profligate part of mankind, and for which he ought to be stigmatised and branded with such an indelible stamp of infamy, that art or even time should be unable to erase or remove from his name or family.' In other words, he probably drugged and raped the girl and in the process transmitted some sort of highly contagious sexual disease.

Although Henry at first offered to take care both of the girl and of the child whom she ultimately bore, he did not keep his word and the girl was left at the mercy of public charity. To make matters worse, the child's wet nurse caught whatever disease had been communicated from the child. It was said that Henry suggested that the child be taken into the Foundling Hospital in London 'to be brought up and maintained at the expenses of public charity, to avoid the charges of it himself'. It was this suggestion that so outraged the compiler of Arabella's memoirs. Sadly, but perhaps fortunately, the child did not survive long enough for this course of action to be taken.

As if his escapade with Arabella Bolton was not enough, Henry went on to father an illegitimate son, also named Henry, in about 1765. This son secured a seat in the Irish Parliament in 1798 and a post in the Irish Government. He was introduced into London Society by the Duchess of Devonshire and his wit made him popular. Lord Byron characterised him as 'the best sayer of good things, and the most epigrammatic conversationalist I have ever met'. Sir Walter Scott called him 'the great London wit' and William Wordsworth also knew him. Henry junior published a collection of poetry in 1820 entitled 'Advice to Julia, a Letter in Rhyme'. In 1827 he published a satirical work entitled 'Crockford House'.

After matriculating from Christ Church, Oxford in 1755, Henry Luttrell entered the army and by 1762 had risen to deputy adjutant-general to the forces in Portugal. He became a major general in 1782 and lived to be the most senior general of the British Army.

Using his close friendship with Lord Bute, First Lord of the Treasury, Lord Irnham managed to get his son elected for the borough of Bossiney in Cornwall in 1768. However, the following year Henry resigned his Cornish seat so that he could stand against the infamous John 'Liberty' Wilkes in the notorious Middlesex by-election. At the poll on 13 April he was defeated by 1,143 votes to 296, but by a resolution of the House of Commons he was two days later declared to have been elected. For some time before the election bets were made on his life; on the polling day he owed his safety to his opponent's friends, and for some days afterwards he 'did not dare to appear in the streets or scarce quit his lodging'. An amusing contemporary caricature by James Gillray depicts 'Mr L- The Irish Arithmetician proving 296 to be more than 1143.'

As a reward for his services to the government in standing against Wilkes, Luttrell was offered the post of adjutant-general of the land forces in Ireland, but this was not enough and two years later he threatened to resign and in 1774 he tried to embroil the government by a complaint that the sheriffs of Middlesex had summoned Wilkes, and not him, to attend in Parliament. From 1774 to 1784, Luttrell sat once again for Bossiney. He represented Plympton Earl in Devon from 1790-4, and from 1817 to his death he was member for Ludgershall in Wiltshire. At the general election in 1783 he was returned in the Irish Parliament for the borough of Old Leighton. In 1776 great happiness came into Henry's life when he married Jane, daughter of George Boyd of Dublin, who was considered to be one of the great beauties of her time.[2] On his father's death in 1787 Henry succeeded to the earldom of Carhampton.

After his accession to the title, Henry is said to have become more arrogant and offensive and on several occasions narrowly escaped the assassin's knife. The episode of the Middlesex by-election had already rendered him 'one of the most unpopular men in England.'[3] In about 1798 he sold his property at Luttrellstown and, a few years later, he purchased the Cobham estate. The purchase was far from straightforward. The estate had ultimately devolved upon three co-heiresses in equal shares and Carhampton had to enter into separate deeds of purchase with each one. It is possible that Carhampton had actually moved to Cobham shortly after disposing of his Irish estates, as it was not unusual for a prospective purchaser to take up residence as a tenant before completing the final formalities of a purchase.

Although Carhampton did little to enlarge the park, he did seek to improve the house and in 1804 the noted architect J.B. Papworth carried out 'a design for east front (gothic) and verandah' for Lord Carhampton. This gothic front can just be seen in an early 19th-century pencil sketch made by a member of the Combe family. Papworth may also have designed the small ornamental dairy which still stands at Cobham Park. Until recently this building had stained glass windows bearing the earl's coat of arms.

Papworth, best known for his work in Cheltenham, also designed Cobham Lodge, which was built on a part of the estate leased to Colonel Joseph Hardy of Waterford. A lease of 1805 stated that the house and land had already been in Hardy's occupation for 'some time past'. It lay to the south of Carhampton's mansion and comprised two lots. The first lot was described as 'All Those two messuages gardens and five fields late part of Cobham Park' and containing a little over 45 acres. The second lot comprised 'All That Messuage or Tenement and Land consisting of seven fields' and containing a little over 94 acres. According to the title deeds, some part of the land leased to Hardy had once formed part of Bottels Farm which had been purchased by John Bridges in 1742. In 1803, Hardy was appointed Inspecting Field Officer of Yeomanry, Cavalry, Drums and Privates in the South Elmbridge Volunteers. This was a volunteer force raised when Napoleon threatened to invade England. In 1810 the Colonel's daughter Catherine died at the age of twenty-two. Seven months later his wife Cassandra died and mother and daughter now lie together in Cobham churchyard.

The loss of his wife and daughter led Hardy to leave Cobham and in 1810 Carhampton entered into negotiations with General Felix Buckley who wished to purchase Cobham Lodge and the five fields comprising 45 acres.[4] Due to problems in clarifying the legal title the sale was not finally completed until 1813 and the property passed out of the original estate.[5] Buckley was Governor of Pendennis Castle and when he died in 1823 he was the oldest living British general, having served in the army for nearly 72 of his 98 years including the bloody battle of Culloden.[6]

In 1804 Lord and Lady Carhampton moved to neighbouring Pains Hill when William Moffat put that estate on the market.[7] The Carhamptons continued to reside at Painshill until their deaths in 1821 and 1831. They are both buried in St Andrew's church, Cobham but there is no monument to their memory.

10

THE LORD MAYOR

On 4 July 1806 Harvey Christian Combe, MP for the City of London and former Lord Mayor of London, signed an agreement with the Earl of Carhampton for the purchase for £30,000 of his Cobham estate. The purchase was to be in two parts with Combe paying £5,000 upon taking possession of the house and a further £11,000 upon having possession of the rest of the estate. The balance of £14,000 was to remain outstanding as a mortgage for a term of five years. A note attached to the Agreement stated that 'The glasses [mirrors] in the House at Cobham to be paid for at the usual price on the Tariff – The Tables under the Glasses to be paid for and also two Cabinets in the Dressing Room – The large curtain to be £25 – The other four £20.' Also included in the sale was 'The small Rick and Stump of Hay in the yard next the Waggon'.[1] The actual sale to Combe was completed in July 1806 and the conveyance lists all the lands included in the sale.[2] From the conveyance it is clear that Combe was already in occupation of both the mansion house and 197 acres of surrounding park and other land. Other lands included in the transaction were those still occupied by Alexander Raby, together with 'Griffins Close and Farm House' occupied by James Gadd, land in the tenure of Richard Chasemore who lived at nearby Chasemore Farm, and various cottages and small pieces of land rented out to local villagers.[3]

The lawyer's bill for handling the purchase includes charges for work undertaken when Combe was considering purchasing nearby Esher Place from the Pelham family. No reason is given for Combe's rejection of Esher but presumably Cobham offered more scope for expansion and greater opportunity to develop an estate to match his growing wealth and social standing. Esher Place was an old estate developed over several centuries around the remnants of a former residence of the Bishop of Winchester. Its position between the river Mole and the growing village of Esher on the busy Portsmouth Road would have allowed little room for growth.[4] By contrast the estate at Cobham was comparatively new, with plenty of room for improvement and expansion should adjoining farms and land become available for purchase. Here the former Lord Mayor could escape the pressures of his busy public life and enjoy the fruits of his labours with his large family in the more comfortable role of a country landowner.

Harvey Christian Combe was the second son of Harvey Combe. His father, a lawyer, owned a sizeable property in the centre of Andover, Hampshire.[5] His elder brother Edmund, a surgeon, had died unmarried in the West Indies in 1782, leaving Harvey junior as the eldest surviving son and heir. Harvey Combe senior, his father and grandfather had all practised law and, although he is believed to have spent some time in his father's office, the legal profession held no attraction for him. It was probably through his mother's family, the Jarmans, and their connections in the sugar refining industry that Harvey junior decided to make a career in the potentially more lucrative brewing industry. His mother's sister Mary had married a wealthy corn-factor, Boyce Tree, and this led Harvey Christian to enter the corn trade at an early age as his uncle's apprentice. Upon completion of his apprenticeship, Boyce Tree took his nephew into the partnership and later made him his heir.

Little is known of Harvey Combe's early life but an undated letter in the family archives provides a glimpse of an emerging strength both of character and physique that were to be his hallmarks in later life. In this letter he reported to his father in dramatic detail how he and a friend had been attacked by a highwayman, somewhere on the southerly outskirts of London:

> The circumstances of taking this Highwayman were not very unlike the other. Mr Curtis & myself were returning from Clapham last Thursday sennight between 7 & 8 – a Man on Horseback bid us stop & coming upon Curtis's Side demanded our money – Curtis gave his but I by endeavouring to save a guinea was not so quick – I took it out of my pocket and got gently off my Seat – I stept over Curtis's Legs and got to the Edge of the Chair – the Man held out his left Hand for ye money into which I put it with my Right Hand – at this Instant I seized the Hand that held the Pistol with my left Hand & griped [*sic*] his Collar with my Right Hand – we came both to the Ground together – he from his Horse & I from the Chair – I never let go my Hold – Curtis imediately [*sic*] jumped out and wrenched the Pistol from his Hand – we secured him & on ye search found another Pistol – that with which he stopt us had four Slugs in it – the other was loaded with small Shot – he was a hardened Dog and discharged from Sr. John Fieldings only the Day before.

Harvey Combe was a life-long enthusiastic supporter of the prize ring and was one of the two umpires in the great fight between 'Gentleman' Humphreys and Daniel Mendoza which took place at the *White Hart* tavern at Stilton on 26 November 1788. One of Combe's obituaries recalled how he had 'found time both for his business and for sport' and was as 'well known at Newmarket as at the ring-side.' When Combe stood for parliament in 1796 he was caricatured as a pugilist and a government newspaper called him 'a man of the world … addicted to gambling and boxing.'

On 9 May 1780, Harvey Christian married his cousin Alice Christian Tree. They were to have 12 children, two of whom died in infancy. With the responsibilities that marriage brought, Combe need to seek out a suitable career for himself and, through his mother's family, he became acquainted with George Shum, also a sugar-refiner with a large business, Shum and Glover, in Lime Street, London. The two subsequently became business partners and life-long friends. The profits to be made in sugar-refining were enormous and it is said that George Shum's father, who 'lived like Scrooge in a narrow court way on the smell of an oil rag and by the heat of a candle', managed to put by £200,000 as his son's inheritance. Following his father's death, George Shum launched forth 'a meteor of City splendour'. He was a good businessman and a close friend of the Prince of Wales, later the Prince Regent, as well as Charles James Fox and the playwright Richard Sheridan. Through Shum, Harvey junior was introduced to each of these colourful personalities and soon became a part of their social circle.

In 1784 the Whig Club had been founded 'to be comprised of Gentlemen, who solemnly pledge themselves to support the Constitution of the Glorious Revolution.' Fox and Sheridan were members together with General Burgoyne, Henry Holland, the architect, and Edmund Burke. Harvey Combe was warmly welcomed into this illustrious company on 7 May 1785, thus associating himself with opposition politics. On that account he was to be six times passed over for the mayoralty. Harvey Combe's political leanings inevitable exposed him to much criticism. This was the period of the broadsheet and lampoon and, with his friend Samuel Whitbread, he was often the victim of caricature and calumny. However, his career and fortune in the brewing trade continued to prosper.

In 1787 Harvey Combe and George Shum purchased the Wood Yard Brewery in the parish of St Martin-in-the-Fields, London. Although sugar-refining is not far removed from brewing, sugar at that time was not permitted for the latter purpose. In the future Combe, together with other brewers such as Whitbread, would be active in lobbying the Government for the use of duty-free sugar in brewing when barley was in short supply. This episode became the subject of a caricature by Gillray. Another member of Combe and Shum's circle was Joseph Delafield, the son of a City merchant and one of Samuel Whitbread's most promising young brewers – the very man they needed to make a success of the brewery trade.

The Wood Yard Brewery took its name from a timber yard that had existed on the site in the 17th century. The brewery had been developed by William Gyfford, a member of an old brewing family who had purchased the business in 1739. When the brewery outgrew its original site, it was moved to new premises just off Tottenham Court Road. By the middle of the 18th century, the Wood Yard Brewery had become the fifth largest in London. Combe's far-sightedness and entrepreneurial skills were clearly demonstrated when he made the move from sugar-refining to brewing. This was an opportune moment. Home brewing was passing out of fashion and there was a growing demand for something stronger than light ales. This was met by porter, a dark brown bitter beer brewed from malt partly charred or browned by drying at a high temperature. It was especially suitable for large-scale commercial brewing and it became highly popular. Much of that success was due to a contract with the Navy to whom the brewery supplied 1,500 barrels of porter in 1778. Together with other well-known London brewers of the day they were popularised in an old drinking song, 'A Pot of Porter Oh':

Again I hope before I die
Of England's can the taste to try
For many a league I'd go about
To take a draught of Gyfford's stout.

In 1785 the Gyfford family's connection with the brewery came to an end and Peter Hammond, one of the surviving partners, was keen to retire. Although Harvey Combe and George Shum were easily able between them to raise the capital sum of £90,000 which was being asked for the Wood Yard Brewery, Hammond decided to retain some interest in the business for his son. Eventually Combe and Shum invested the sum of £26,000 each into acquiring the business. Their friend Delafield invested a further £23,000 and the remainder of the capital remained in the name of Hammond's son. However, when Hammond's son was declared bankrupt a few years later, his partners were able to buy him out of the business.

Immediately following their purchase of the brewery, the progressive partners invested in the purchase of a new steam engine from the famous company of Boulton and Watt at Soho, Birmingham. The Wood Yard Brewery was the sixth in the country to order one of the new engines. During the first ten years of trading the partnership of Shum, Combe, Delafield more than doubled its value. Shum became a director of the Phoenix Assurance Company and gave up a quarter of his interest to his son, who was also called George. The consumption of porter reached its peak about this time and it was decided to rebuild the brewery. A contemporary commentator observed that Combe was then reputed to be worth upwards of £100,000. In his late 40s, he was already one of the most successful brewers in the country, a respected public figure, a fearless orator and a patron the arts. It was said that 'his acquaintance was wide and his integrity unassailable. Of easy bearing, he could deal as effectively and courteously with the rawest stable boy as he could with the Prince of Wales himself.'

Having established himself in the brewing industry, Harvey Combe became a member of the Brewers' Company and represented Aldgate ward from 1790 to 1817. In 1805 he became the Company's Master. From 1791 to 1792 he served as Sheriff of London and Middlesex and in 1793 he became Governor of the Irish Society. This society had been formed to promote friendship and understanding between the two peoples as well as providing relief of the Irish poor.

In 1796 Combe commenced his political career by being elected as Member of Parliament for the City of London. Following his election, his politics soon became evident. Although he claimed 'to be attached personally to no man, nor to have any prejudice against any of the members of administration', he did clearly ally himself with his friend, the radical Charles James Fox. Combe also supported his friend and fellow brewer Samuel Whitbread who was a passionate supporter of reform in areas such as religious and civil rights, the abolition of the slave-trade, and the establishment of a national educational system. Combe spoke out against the Tory Prime Minster, William Pitt, for unnecessarily taking the country into the war with France. In 1797 Combe voted for parliamentary reform. He also advocated regulation of food prices and sought tax relief for retail shopkeepers. In 1798 Combe opposed the renewed suspension of *habeas corpus* and, in the following year, he voted against the Irish union.

In 1799 Harvey Combe finally became Lord Mayor of London. His year of office opened brilliantly with the customary banquet in November. The new Lord Mayor could well afford to make a splash. His business was doing well and porter was selling at 4½d a quart. It was during Combe's year as Lord Mayor that the City honoured Admiral Lord Nelson following the Battle of the Nile. They presented Nelson with a sword to mark the occasion and the Persian traveller, Mirza Abu Taleb Khan, recorded his impressions of this important social event:

> On my entering the apartment, the Lord Mayor took me by the hand and introduced me to the Lady Mayoress who was dressed as fine as a queen and seated with great pomp on a superb sofa. In compliment to me as a foreigner, her ladyship rose from her seat. The dinner having been announced, the Lord Mayor again took my hand and led me to a table that was raised a step or two above the others. His lordship sat on the right of the Lady Mayoress and on his right hand were seated Lord Coventry, Lord Spencer, Lord Nelson and several other noblemen.

Taleb Khan later described one of Harvey Combe's daughters who was present on this occasion as 'the bright moon surrounded with brilliant stars'.

As Lord Mayor, Harvey Combe sat in his robes of office for a portrait by John Opie, R.A. A friendship sprang up between the painter and his patron and Opie was invited to dine with the Irish Society one evening in March 1807. The room where they dined was large and cold and Opie drank more than he should to warm himself. When he left the event he found that that there had been a heavy snowfall. He could not afford a carriage and had to walk home. The next day he took to his bed and died a few days later.

Two years after bestowing the honours of the City on Admiral Lord Nelson, there followed the Peace of Amiens, designed by Napoleon to enable him to build up his strength against this country. It became popular again at this time to cross the Channel and London society flocked to Paris, some in the interest of peace, but many others simply out of curiosity. Combe made the visit in the company of Charles James Fox, Lord Erskine and Richard Sheridan. There were many who still distrusted Napoleon and these included the popular caricaturist, James Gillray. The visit by Combe his Whig friends formed the subject of his cartoon, English Patriots bowing at the Shrine of Despotism. Combe reported on the visit to his son in a letter from Reims dated 17 August 1802:

> My Dear Harvey,
>
> If I been aware how easily to you and us it might have been done I should have preferred you very much to have come over with us to Calais and to have returned by the same vessel which set off on her Return the Evening

on which we left that Town in the morning – I don't think you would have found it disagreeable to have spent the second day for Arthur O'Connor would have had great Pleasure in taking care of you and that he is a very agreeable Gentlemanly man even my Fellow Travellers who are great aristocrats acknowledge – We are now about Two Hundred miles from that Town and it is impossible for any Country in the World to exhibit the same space of uninterrupted good Tillage – every Inch of Land seems occupied – the Crops are abundant and the Harvest is very fine indeed they have had no Rain here these three months – It is curious to observe from Laon to this to this Place the various Vineyards that are planted at the Sides of the Hills but also the Vines are very healthful. There is scarcely any Fruit – the same Frosts in June which destroyed our apples and other things have done irreparable Injury to the Wines – they are tied to sticks about three feet or three & ½ high – We got here only this morning and have not yet visited any of the famous ones but we shall in a Day or two – We have passed thro' some very pretty Towns particularly Combray and Laon but we stopped no where but to sleep – the first night after Calais at Bethune – the second at St Quentin – last night at Berry au Dac – nothing material has happened to us except one over Turn and a wheel broke by the hard driving of a Postilion who almost swung us over in turning a corner – our Route is uncertain because the Gentleman we expect to meet here is at Paris – he will probably be here tomorrow – I hope every body and every thing are well – I assure you I don't like to be so far off lest any Accident of any kind may happen – give my love to Mr & Mrs Delafield – I would write to your Uncle but this Letter to you will do as well – and the same apology will serve to Mrs Thorp to whom you will always remember me – I will write to you again before I leave this Place – but at any Rate just write to me on the Tuesday or Friday next after you receive this directed -

     a Monsr. H.C. Combe a' Paris –
     restant au Poste
Just to say, as I hope you will, that all is well
Yrs affectionately
H.C.C.
Your letter must be paid for in Lombard Street.

On 2 September Joseph Farringdon met Combe in the Louvre and recorded that Combe had said 'whatever might be thought of the modern French Exhibition, it was very superior to what was seen in England'. The artist Opie who was with Combe and his circle, immediately felt led to spring to the defence of British art.[6]

The following year Britain and France were at war again. Britain's troubles at this time were made worse by poor harvests which had raised the price of wheat, leaving the mass of the people on the brink of famine. Even in normal times the country did not grow enough grain for the subsistence of the nation. As the bread famine grew worse, the hungry mob smashed the windows of bakers and stormed the mills and premises of corn merchants. In his house in Mark Lane, John Bolland, who sold hops to Combe's brewery, was besieged by an infuriated crowd. As chief magistrate, Combe was soon on the scene and without recourse to force dispersed the mob, the good sense he showed on this occasion becoming the subject of a eulogistic tract 'Firmness in Danger'. The Court of Common Council on his retirement as Lord Mayor passed a resolution commending 'that rare and salutary and noble union of wisdom and courage, and of justice with clemency which he displayed during the late disturbance from the scarcity of corn and for which his name deserves to be recorded in the annals of our history as the friend of the poor, the guide of the ignorant, the bloodless subduer of the rash and tumultuous, the guardian of the peace, property and lives of his fellow citizens, the preserver of the general tranquillity of the kingdom, and a magistrate who consecrated the legal exercise of power by the most amiable feelings of humanity.'

When shortly after the end of his year of office as Lord Mayor invasion by the French seemed a real threat, Combe became a Captain of the Aldgate Volunteers. Two years later, he became Colonel of the Loyal London Volunteers, a rank he retained for the next six years.

Harvey Christian Combe was held in wide esteem and was on intimate terms with many of the most famous men of his day. He was often to be seen at the card tables of the fashionable clubs of London and there is a legend that some of Combe's public houses were won at cards from Lord Portman. Combe, although playing for high stakes, avoided too much drink at the table and kept a clear head. Unlike many of his circle, he never gambled beyond his means. His friend Fox was notorious for the sums he lost but once when he won a considerable sum from Combe he is said to have exclaimed 'Bravo, old Mashtubs, I will never drink any porter but yours', to which Combe replied 'Sir, I wish every other scoundrel in London would say the same.' [7]

Combe was also highly regarded by the Royal Family and he gave an annual 'Brewhouse dinner of beefsteaks' in their honour. This was attended at least twice by the Prince of Wales and his brother the Duke of York. Of a dinner held in June 1808, the Star newspaper reported that the fare consisted of 'rump steaks cooked upon an iron plate on the stoker's fire, and conveyed on a new malt shovel to the company, who partook of them in the brewhouse, a short distance from the fire. Their table was a hop sack, and they ate off wooden trenchers; salads were in wooden bowls, and everything in the rough implements of the Brewhouse.' The Prince of Wales, the Duke and Duchess of York, and the Duke of Cambridge were the principle guests. 'Their Royal Highness arrived at a quarter before seven o'clock; they were received by the Alderman and Mrs Combe, who conducted them to the table. Five rumps of beef were provided, and a butcher attended to cut the prime steaks, which were served up in the finest way possible. The rest of the company consisted of the Duke of Argyle, the Earl of Lauderdale, Lords Erskine, Yarmouth and Kinnaird, Ladies Kinnaird and A. Smith; Mr. B. Paget and Mr H, Combe. The only beverage they partook of was the porter of the Brewhouse. The company left the Brewhouse about half past seven, highly gratified with their entertainment. A crowd of persons assembled round the gateway and greeted the Princes with loud huzzas. The company proceeded to Alderman Combe's residence in Great Russell Street, Bloomsbury, where they partook of several courses of delicacies. The Princes left about half past nine, the rest of the company remained till eleven.' Combe's friend Sheridan was another regular guest on these occasions.

The Wood Yard Brewery went from strength to strength and in 1816 the partnership purchased the brewery of Hollingsworth & Co. in Southwark, thereby adding 21 more public houses into their trade. The following year Combe's eldest son joined the brewery at the age of twenty-two.

Harvey Combe's business affairs and public office allowed him little time for developing his new estate at Cobham and, save for the purchase of 14 acres of copyhold land in the neighbouring parish of Little Bookham, he seems to have done little to enlarge the estate.[8] Combe needed to consolidate what he had acquired and make it profitable. One Cobham property that he did purchase in 1811 was an old cottage known as 'The Garden House' that stood immediately across the road from the entrance to Cobham Park.[9] Although it was in 1812 that Combe obtained permission from the Lord of the Manor to demolish this and the other copyhold properties which he had acquired upon his purchase of the estate from Lord Carhampton, it was left to his son to develop these sites.

Documents which survive from this time include Harvey Combe's cheque book counterfoils for the period June 1799 to May 1801, and his pocket book containing details of his personal income and expenditure during the period 1812-17.[10] Unfortunately, the entries are extremely brief and reveal little about his life at Cobham. This book also contains 'An Account in Cash with W. Elson beginning 1st Sept. 1812.' Elson was Combe's Estate Bailiff at this time.

More enlightening are two volumes of accounts covering the period 1806 to 1817 which provide interesting glimpses into the management of the estate and the farm.[11] One of the first entries is the payment of £4 10s. for six men who spent five day cleaning the canals in October 1806. The canals were presumably the water features created by John Bridges and which were later made into the present lake. The men employed to clear the canals were also allowed one pot of beer per day. Other work involved 'embanking the meadow', presumably to stop flooding from the adjoining river Mole, and 'pulling down the house in the park'. This last entry related to the demolition of one of the small copyhold cottages that still stood within the park. A ledger entry made in 1808 records how Combe paid £2 8s.8d. for 'Digging 73 yards of Gravel at the Tartar'. The parish gravel pits were found on the edge of the Fairmile Common on Tartar Hill and presumably Combe, unlike his predecessor John Bridges, obtained the necessary permission for this action. A major landscape contribution to estate management policy at this time was tree-planting. The famous agricultural improver Thomas Coke of Holkham was nicknamed 'King

Pine' for planting innumerable pine trees on the sandy soils of his Norfolk estate and perhaps it was he who encouraged Combe to plant 1,000 fir trees at Cobham in 1810. This is a very large number for the size of the estate and they were planted as a cash crop given the increasing use of soft timber for building. Forty limes and 100 spruces followed in 1811.

The accounts reveal the usual seasonal payments for work on the farm such as ploughing, harvesting and threshing. In August 1807 Mills, who kept the *Waggon and Horses* ale house across the road from the park, was paid £2 8s.7d. for beer for the 'Hay and Harvest'. An additional payment of £2 3s.0¼d. was made for 'Sundries for Harvest Home Supper'. The following year liquid refreshment for the harvest workers was provided by Joseph Stedman, who later established the Cobham Brewery at Street Cobham. In 1810 Stedman was paid £3 for providing refreshments both for the 'Harvest Home & Ice House'. The ice house, which still stands in the park, was an early form of refrigeration. It was filled each year with ice brought up from the lake and packed in straw; the completion of this task merited beer and bread all round for those involved.

The sale and purchase of livestock features prominently in the accounts. Stock was usually purchased at local fairs such as those held at Chertsey, Dorking, Guildford and Kingston. In 1807 £16 10s. was paid for 'a white red spotted cow and calf at Ewell Fair'. Stock was usually driven to London to be sold at Smithfield market although sometimes individual animals were sold to local people. Sheep-rearing was the major emphasis of the farm and in July 1809 Combe exchanged notes with his neighbour, Lord Somerville, who kept a famous flock of Merino sheep at his farm on the Fairmile. Somerville was on close terms with another famous sheep breeder, 'Farmer' George III. On 16 July Combe made a note that he had agreed to hire a particular ram from Somerville 'for the season at 60 guineas and then pay the hire or buy the ram outright at 150 guineas'. In 1810 Somerville was paid £63 for the use of 'Spanish Ram'.[12] The estate accounts contain regular payments for the washing and shearing of the flock. Payments were made to the men, or boys, whose job it was to drive cattle and sheep to and from local markets.

Some of the more unusual occupations on the estate were those of the mole catcher and the man paid £10 4s. for 'Digging out 10,200 ant hills'. Another man was paid for killing 30 rats at 2½d. each. Women were regularly employed in weeding the fields and assisting with the harvest. They were also employed on a casual basis, such as in 1808 when Sarah Colton was paid 13 shillings for 'picking Turnips'. From time to time quantities of dung were purchased from local sources for manuring the fields and lime for neutralising the soil was burned in local lime kilns.

In addition to the wages of estate employees, the accounts also show regular payments to local tradesmen such as Sheryer the blacksmith, Peto the miller, Parsons the wheelwright, Walker the harness and collar maker, Trimmings the bricklayer and Thomas Caulder, who in 1809 was paid 14s. 9d. for 'Candles & Sulphur'. The implements and tools for farming were a necessary expense and in 1806 Combe paid £2 3s. for 'a new drill plough'.[13]

Like most other small rural communities at this time Cobham had its own 'market economy' with local land owners and farmers trading amongst themselves. In 1810 Combe paid £16 10s.9d. for 4½ acres of turnips from Major Abingdon of Leigh Hill House which stood overlooking the river on the site now occupied by Leigh Place estate. In the same year he purchased 'Faggots, Hurdles & etc.' from John Balchin who lived at nearby Cedar House. 'Hurdles and stakes' were sold to Crawter & Sons, Cobham land agents and surveyors. Another of Combe's neighbours with whom he did business from time to time was his old friend Richard Brinsley Sheridan, who was living at Polesden Lacy in Great Bookham.

The accounts also remind us that this was a period of high taxation. The wars with France had to be paid for. Taxation was introduced on a great variety of things and for Combe in 1808 these included land, windows, male servants, two wheeled carriages, riding horses and dogs. Travel could also be expensive as it was necessary to pay fees to use the newly improved turnpikes such as the Portsmouth Road.

It was as well for Combe that his main source of income was the brewery. Farming was hardly profitable at this period and initially the farm was run at a loss. However, in 1810 a profit of just over £1,000 was achieved and in the following years income of about £800.

Throughout this period Harvey Combe remained active within the House of Commons. In December 1806 it was reported that the king had considered him for a knighthood.[14] Although brewing remained his primary business venture, in 1805 Combe became a director of the Globe Insurance Company, a position that he held until his death. One of Combe's less successful business enterprises was an investment in a London theatre. The Theatre Royal, Drury Lane was destroyed by fire in 1809 and, in 1812, Combe became a member of its new management committee which was led by another brewer, his friend Samuel Whitbread. Already over £500,000 in debt, the theatre was in danger of going out of business. None of the committee had any theatrical experience and decided to sub-let the theatre to a professional, Samuel Arnold. Unfortunately, Arnold was unable to make it pay and, in 1815, the shareholders elected a new committee. Combe appears to have stood back from the venture at this stage and decided against joining the new committee whose members included Lord Byron. Combe appears to have acted wisely as the business continued to fail, leading Whitbread to commit suicide.

From about 1812 onwards Combe was increasingly impeded by illness. He suffered from a paralytic complaint and made his last recorded parliamentary speech in 1814. In June 1817, as the result of 'a wanton and cruel insult' inflicted upon him when he attended Common Hall, Harvey Combe suffered a debilitating stroke which led him to retire both from public life and the brewery affairs. According to one report, 'Without losing a day he resigned his seat in Parliament, his aldermanic gown, and all his civic offices, including membership of Court of the Fishmongers' Company.' The effects of the stroke are visible from the handwriting in his account books at this time. It was not the first time that his rivals had intrigued against him. Twenty years earlier, some aldermen had sought to put him aside as Lord Mayor for a year.

Harvey Combe was only to have one year to enjoy family life at his Surrey retreat following his retirement from all his public offices. He died on 4 July 1818 and was buried in the imposing family mausoleum in the churchyard on the north side of St Andrew's church at Cobham.[15] Combe's widow, Alice, lived on for another ten years. She died on 27 October 1828 and was finally laid to rest beside her husband.

It is written of Harvey Christian Combe that 'no brewer, except perhaps [his] contemporary, Samuel Whitbread, better demonstrated the social and political range of London's super-rich brewing fraternity in the Georgian period'.[16] An obituary in the *Gentleman's Magazine* described Harvey Christian Combe as 'a kind husband, and an indulgent father; firm and warmly zealous in his friendships'. He left an estate valued at £140,000. Having contributed to charities and worthy causes all his life, Harvey Combe left his estate to his family. To each of his three sons, he left £10,000 – his youngest son, Charles James Fox, having already received that sum on a promissory note which had just left him with a marble bust of his famous namesake. The second son, Boyce, after starting a career as an insurance broker, became a London magistrate in which capacity he served for 30 years. It was left to the eldest son, Harvey, not only to follow his father into the business but also take up the reigns as the second generation at Cobham and consequently consolidate, develop and enlarge the estate.

YOUNG HARVEY

Harvey Combe junior, or 'Young Harvey' as he is still affectionately known (and as he is called in this chapter), was 34 years old when his father died and, although he had already assumed a measure of responsibility for the estate when the Alderman had suffered his debilitating stroke, it was only now that he could take control and be admitted as a full partner in the Brewery. Young Harvey inherited a share worth £85,000 in a business that had become one of the country's leading breweries, ranking alongside those of Reid and Watney with which it was eventually to merge. But Young Harvey's inheritance was two-fold as he also inherited the valuable family estate at Cobham.

Despite the fact that Cobham Park had for many years been the most important estate in the village, none of its former occupants had taken much interest in local affairs. It is true that Lord Carhampton occasionally attended meetings of the Cobham Vestry but this was probably more a measure to protect his own interests than an act generated by real public spirit. Harvey Christian's role in the local community had been limited first by his commitments in the City and then by his declining health. However, for Young Harvey, as the second generation at Cobham, the inheritance of an established country estate opened up a new world as a member of the landed gentry. Regency England was at its peak. Napoleon had been defeated at Waterloo in 1815 and Europe was at peace.

F.M.L. Thompson has written, 'The landed gentry came in a bewildering variety of shapes and sizes, but contemporaries were confident that they formed a reasonably homogeneous group, the solid core of the landed interest, mainstay of the hunting field and backbone of the resident magistracy which managed the country … they were the untitled aristocracy.'[1] The local community were undoubtedly ready to receive Young Harvey as his father's son and relieved to see that some continuity was being established in the occupancy of Cobham Park which had become the principal house in the village. His late father's 'new money' soon became 'old money' and, although he remained an active senior partner in the brewery until his death, his growing position within the ranks of the county gentry brought demands of another sort. On 31 January 1831 Young Harvey was appointed Sheriff of Surrey.[2] To maintain his new lifestyle as a country gentleman, Young Harvey improved and enlarged Cobham Park mansion and a contemporary county history has the following brief description of the house during his ownership:

> ... a handsome and substantial building, nearly square, with a neat portico erected in the place of a veranda. The good saloon, with coved and ornamental ceiling, was turned into a billiard room, and the library and other convenient apartments were embellished with busts and pictures.[3]

Young Harvey had probably added the portico, and the billiard room would have been more useful to the bachelor squire. The architect J.B. Papworth had also added a conservatory in the fashionable 'Gothick' style. In the park Young Harvey reshaped the formal canal, created a century earlier by John Bridges, into an irregularly shaped lake that mirrored the garden façade of the house.

The ten-yearly census returns from 1841 provide glimpses into the big house and how it was run giving Young Harvey's occupation as 'Independent'. This seems to be more a statement of gentry aspiration than fact as he was still living on income from the brewery. Sharing the house with him were his unmarried sisters Frances and Mary Anne together with a total of 12 domestic servants. In 1851 the enumerator recorded Harvey Combe as a 'Brewer occupying 800 Acres of Land with 30 Labourers'. It is strange that he should revert to this description rather than 'land owner'. Perhaps by this time he felt secure enough in his new role to acknowledge the sourse of his income. It also supports the statement of Herbert Pocket in Charles Dicken's *Great Expectations*: 'It is indisputable that while you cannot possibly be genteel and bake, you can be as genteel as never was and brew.' By 1851 Frances was dead and Young Harvey and Mary Anne were sharing the house together with an unmarried niece named Henrietta and nephew Richard, who was to inherit half his uncle's share in the brewery. At this time the census provides the occupations of the various servants and these are a butler, a footman, a page, a housekeeper, a cook, two housemaids, a kitchen maid, three grooms and two gardeners. Ten years later young Harvey was dead and Mary Anne was at the house with assorted relatives and a staff of ten servants. Henry Coldman, who had been working for the family in 1841, was still there as butler 20 years later. His wife became cook in 1851. Clearly the Coldmans were irreplaceable.

Another very visible reminder of the Combe family's presence in Cobham was the large family mausoleum erected following Harvey Christian's death and which still dominates the parish churchyard. The family had their own private pew in the church from shortly after their arrival in the village; on 3 December 1829 a 'Faculty for Private Entrance to the Pew of Harvey Combe, Esq. in the Parish Church of Cobham, Surrey' was granted by the diocesan authorities.[4] In 1852 Young Harvey purchased the advowson of Cobham from Henry Weston for the sum of £800. This gave him the right to present, or appoint, the vicar of Cobham, a right that still remains with the family. This purchase would have been made with more than just the spiritual state of the village in mind. The pulpit was an important element of control in rural society and Young Harvey needed to be able to appoint a man who would support the landed view and preach the gospel of social hierarchy both from the pulpit and in his pastoral work around the parish.

59 'Young Harvey' built the stable block at Cobham Park in the 1840s. The keystone over the arch is from the Wood Yard Brewery in London and was perhaps a reminder both to Combe and his visitors of the source of the family's fortunes.

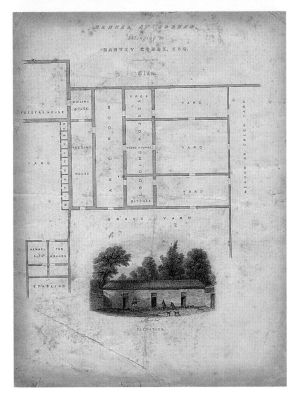

60 'Kennel at Cobham belonging to Harvey Combe, Esq.' An engraving of *c.*1840, published in R. Ackermann's Eclipse Sporting Gallery.

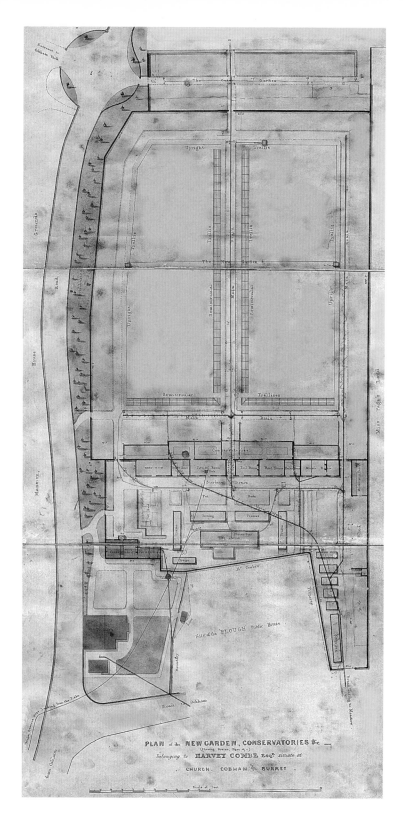

61 Plan of the model kitchen garden at Cobham Park laid out by 'Young Harvey', from a survey of 1855.

62 The glasshouse at Cobham Park kitchen garden in 1899.

63 'Young Harvey' purchased the former Cobham Rectory in the 1840s and replaced it with Rose Lodge, seen here in this 19th-century watercolour.

64 Cobham Park tenants and neighbours celebrated Queen Victoria's wedding in 1840 at Downside (now Down) Farm.

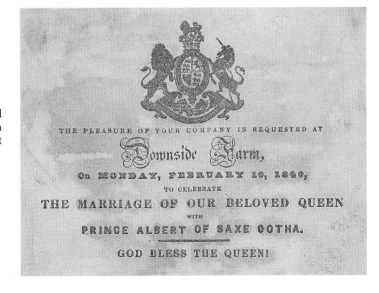

COBHAM PARK, COBHAM, SURREY.

FIRST PERIODICAL SALE.

A CATALOGUE

OF PURE BRED

SHORT-HORNED CATTLE,

BELONGING TO HARVEY COMBE, ESQ.,

Which will be Sold by Auction,

WITHOUT RESERVE,

BY MR. H. STRAFFORD,

AT THE DOWNSIDE FARM,

ON

WEDNESDAY, THE 5TH DAY OF JUNE, 1850.

THE SALE TO COMMENCE AT ONE O'CLOCK.

Cobham is 5 miles from the Esher and Walton Stations on the South Western Railway, from which places Stock may be conveyed by rail to any part of the Kingdom.

Catalogues may be had on application to Mr. J. P. Giles, Downside Farm, Cobham; and of Mr. STRAFFORD, 3, Camden Villas, Camden Town.

LONDON:
PRINTED AT THE "MARK LANE EXPRESS" OFFICE,
24, NORFOLK STREET, STRAND.

65 'Young Harvey's' herd of Short-Horned Cattle received national recognition. This sale catalogue is from 1850.

66 After the death of 'Young Harvey' his sister Mary Anne completed a scheme he had started to bring clean water to the people of Downside. When the pump was erected it was described as a 'noble pump free to all inhabitants who now enjoy the blessing of plenty and good water which they had long and sorely felt the want of the little they could obtain being almost unfit for use.' The pump stands by the entrance to St Michael's Chapel, overlooking the common.

67 (above)   Charles James Fox Combe (1797-1875), son of Harvey Christian Combe and godson of Charles James Fox and Richard Sheridan.

68 (above right)   Eliza Combe née Roberts, wife of Charles James Fox Combe and mother of Charles Combe who inherited the Cobham estate from his uncle 'Young Harvey'.

69 (right)   Charles Combe, Charles James Fox Combe, Boyce Albert Combe.

70 *The Siege of Kooshab.* Charles Combe is featured in this painting of the celebrated cavalry charge of 1857.

71 (left)   Charles and Marianne Combe in 1861.

72 (above)   Cobham Park: the south front. From a photograph taken in the 1860s.

73 Cobham Park: the north front. From a photograph taken in the 1860s.

74 Marianne Combe, from a photograph taken in *c*.1870.

75 Percy, Grace, Charlie and Evelyn Combe. A delightful early seaside tintype taken in the early 1870s.

76 A remarkable photograph of four generations taken in 1899 and showing Mrs Charles Inglis, Marianne Combe née Inglis, Grace Ethel Deare née Combe and Dorothy Deare.

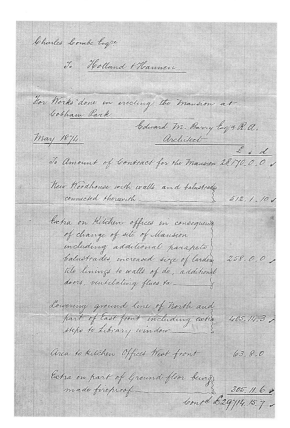

77 Holland & Hammer's account for the building
of the new Cobham Park mansion to the designs
of Edward Barry, R.A.

78 Cobham Park: entrance
gate and lodge in 1899.

79 Cobham Park: the south
front in 1899.

80 Cobham Park: the north front across the lake in 1899.

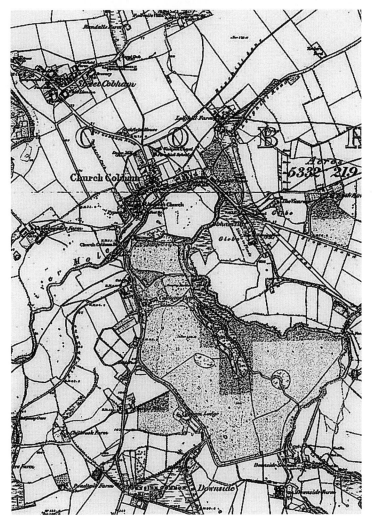

81 This extract from the 1870 OS map shows the extent of Cobham Park and its relationship to the village of Cobham.

82 Cobham Park: the Broadwater on the river Mole, looking south, in 1899. John Bridges had widened this section of the river in the 18th century to improve the view from the house.

83 Cobham Park: the Broadwater looking north in 1899.

84 This photograph of 1899 shows the water wheel which was installed by the Suffolk firm of Whitmore & Binyon to pump water to the new house.

85 After the water wheel was installed in 1884 Charles Combe wrote to one of his sons that the mill pond would provide a 'capital bathing place'.

86 Cobham Park: the lawn and weeping birch in 1899.

87 Footbridge and cattle in Cobham Park in 1899.

88 Cattle in the river Mole below Downside Bridge in 1899.

89 The bridge on the bridle way from Cobham Tilt to Downside in 1899.

90 Cobham Park Stud Farm, *c.*1879. Here was bred 'Blair Athol, the Blaze-faced King of Cobham', one of the most famous racehorses of the 19th century.

91 Cobham Park Stud Farm sale in 1879. The bearded gentleman is probably Charles Combe. HRH The Prince of Wales, later Edward VII, came here with his mistress Lillie Langtry to buy horses.

92   Charles Combe and his children at Cobham Park, Easter 1886.

93   The Hewitts of Spencer House (now Ham Manor) at a picnic in Cobham Park in 1890. The Hewitt family were close friends of the Combe family and there are a number of photographs of various members of the family in the Combe albums.

94 A posed but informal photograph of 1889 showing Charles Combe with Grace Ethel, Percy, Harvey Edward, Florence and Gertrude. Charles Combe has hung his hat on the walking stick held by Harvey Edward and Florence appears to be about to remove her younger brother's cap.

95 A delightfully informal group of Grace Ethel Combe, Evelyn Combe, Gertrude Combe and Florence Combe playing with a dog at Cobham Park.

96 Ethel and Evelyn Combe in the conservatory at Cobham Park in 1891.

97 Evelyn, Gertrude, Florence and Grace Ethel Combe outside the conservatory at Cobham Park in 1899.

98 Putting in Cobham Park in 1895. The identity of the two young men is not known.

99 Percy, Gwendolyn, Kenneth and Florence Combe playing croquet in Cobham Park in 1899.

100 Gertrude, Edith and baby Harold in 1899.

101 Charles Harvey Combe, 'Charlie', outside the Cobham Park billiards room in 1899.

102 Charlie and his brother Percy on their return from their world tour in 1884.

103 Charlie and Percy Combe with John Samuel Spry in San Francisco in 1884.

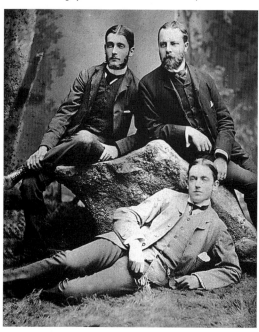

104 A rare informal photograph of Mrs Combe sitting on the doorstep of Cobham Park in 1899.

105 Aunts, nieces and nephews – a wonderful period photograph taken at Christmas 1912 and showing (left to right) Amy Combe, Patrick & Betty Combe (in dog cart), Dorothy Combe, Joyce Radcliffe (on donkey), Gertrude Radcliffe née Combe, Rachel, John & Rupert Serocold (in donkey cart), Gwendolyn Serocold née Combe and Florence Combe.

106 Kenneth Combe in the billiards room at Cobham Park in 1899.

107 Nurse with baby Harold, son of Grace Ethel and Henry Foulkes Deare, at Cobham Park in 1899.

108 (above) 'Faircroft', Between Streets, Cobham in 1899. This was the first home after their marriage of Grace Ethel Combe and Henry Foulkes Deare.

109 (right) Charles Combe was one of the chief promoters of the scheme to build Cobham's first Village Hall in 1888. Other supporters included Matthew Arnold, who lived at Painshill Cottage.

110 (below) Cobham Village Hall, *c.*1910.

Dated 1st March, 1888.

THOMAS HENRY BENNETT, Esq.,

TO

CHARLES COMBE, Esq., and OTHERS.

𝕮𝖔𝖓𝖛𝖊𝖞𝖆𝖓𝖈𝖊 of a Piece of Land at Cobham, Surrey, for the site of a Village Hall.

JAMES BELL,
Kingston-on-Thames.

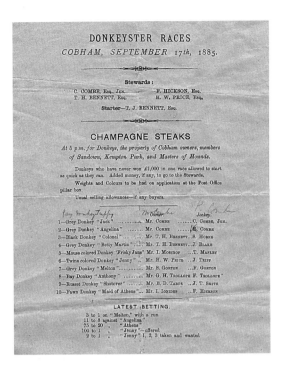

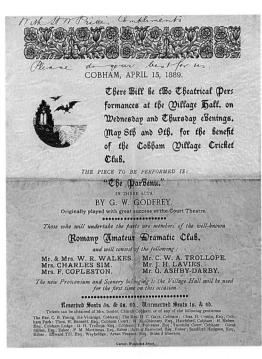

111 (above)   Cobham's 'Donkeyster Races', held in 1885, were supported by the Combes and other leading families in Cobham.

112 (above right)   In 1889 a theatrical performance was held at Cobham Village Hall for the benefit of Cobham Village Cricket Club, one of the many local causes supported by Charles Combe.

113 (right)   Cobham Village Cricket Club Annual Dinner, 1889.

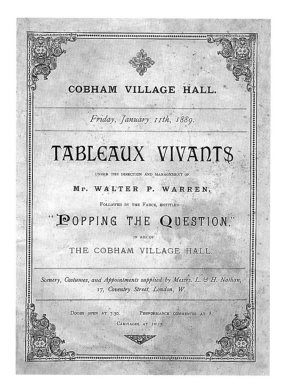

114 Members of the Combe family took part in the Tableaux Vivants held at Cobham Village Hall in 1889.

115 Cobham Brass Band was another local cause supported by Charles Combe. He made the band a loan to purchase new equipment and uniforms.

116 Yachting was one of Charles Combe's greatest pleasures and he had his own steam yacht, the *Dotterel*, seen here in 1899.

117 Charles Combe junior fishing from the *Dotterel* during a visit to the Scilly Isles in 1899.

118 The crew of the *Dotterel* in 1889.

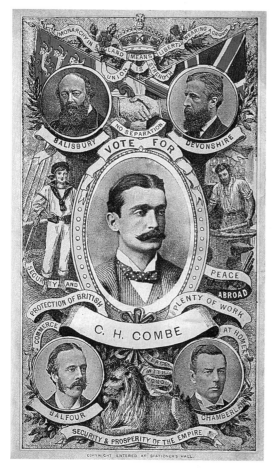

119 (above left)   Charles Combe, 'Squire of Cobham' in 1880.

120 (above)   Marianne Combe in 1880.

121 (left)   Charles Harvey Combe was MP for the Chertsey Division of Surrey from 1892-97 when he stood down due to ill health.

122 This is probably Joseph Potter who is recorded as the Lodge Keeper at Cobham in the 1891 census.

123 William Bacon, a gardener at Cobham Park, was a veteran of the Crimean War.

124 This photograph of *c*.1900 shows a Laundry cottage built by Charles Combe in 1882. The group outside are probably Thomas Potter, the Cobham Park butler, and his wife who lived here together, Charlotte Anthoness, who was in charge of the laundry, and her assistants.

125 William Bacon at work in Cobham Park in 1899.

126 Watering horses at Downside (now Down) Farm, *c.*1895.

127 One of Charles Combe's prize Alderney bulls at Downside Farm, seen here with his farm manager William Gale.

128 The porch at Cobham Park decorated for Mafeking Day, 1900. The man standing on the steps is believed to be Vicomte de la Brosse, a friend of the family.

129 The porch at Cobham Park decorated to welcome home Kenneth Combe from South Africa in 1901.

130 A house party at Cobham Park, Christmas 1910.

131 Alice Ethel Cushney, second wife of Charles Combe, was considered to be a great beauty of her day. She made it a condition of her marriage to Combe that he purchased her former husband's estate at Painshill.

132 Charles Combe in the ballroom at Painshill with members of his family in 1909.

133　Cobham Park: drawing room, *c.*1930.

134　Cobham Park: drawing room, *c.*1930.

135 Cobham Park: entrance hall, *c*.1930.

136 Charles Combe ('Charlie') at billiards in Cobham Park, *c*.1930.

137 Dorothy Mabel Combe née Livingstone, wife of Charles Harvey Combe.

138 Tea in the nursery at Cobham Park. Charles Harvey Christian Combe is seen here with his sisters Rosemary and Anne and their nurse in the early 1930s.

139 Charles Harvey Christian Combe (1926-83).

140 Elizabeth Ann Shiers Combe née Lowe.

In 1834 the following lines appeared in a humorous poem in the *New Monthly Magazine & Literary Journal*:

> Let lofty mansions great men keep –
> I have no wish to rob 'em –
> Not courtly Claremont, Esher's steep,
> *Nor Squire Combe's at Cobham.*[5]

Hunting and horse racing were two of the particular pleasures of 'Squire Combe' at Cobham. An engraving of 1841 shows the kennels which he had built to house his hounds. Young Harvey was also Master of both the Old Berkeley and Old Berks Hunts for many years and was a familiar figure in hunting country which then extended without interruption from Scratch Wood, seven miles from his place of business, as far as Cirencester in Gloucestershire, a distance of nearly eighty miles. When railway mania gripped the country in the second quarter of the 19th century, this hitherto unspoilt stretch of countryside was divided by the London and Birmingham Railway which had been founded in 1832 by a group of gentlemen including brewers and bankers. In 1838 a locomotive, designed and built by Robert Stephenson, was named 'Harvey Combe' in honour of 'one so well known in the area'. This locomotive was used in the construction of the London and Birmingham Railway near Berkhamsted. In the late 1840s Young Harvey rebuilt the stables at Cobham Park. The keystone over the stable yard entrance carries the inscription 'Wood Yard Brewhouse 1849'. This inscription may have come from the London brewery and be a statement of the origins of the family's fortunes.

When Young Harvey inherited the Cobham estate it comprised some 400 acres. In addition to improvements which could be made to the house, the estate and the farm, there were also many opportunities for expansion. However, the Napoleonic Wars were immediately followed by a period of severe depression. A run of bad harvests and a shortage of work for those returning from the war eventually led to a period of social unrest. In the countryside this found expression in the Swing Riots of the 1820s and 1830s. For many farmers this period proved disastrous and it was fortunate that Young Harvey with his share in the brewery was not dependent upon the farm for his income. The 1840s brought more concern and upheaval in advance of the repeal of the Corn Laws. But for those who could ride the storm there emerged a new style of gentleman farmer who would both ride to hounds and spend a day sorting the sheep for clipping. They were concerned with 'scientific farming' and agricultural improvements and they included Young Harvey among their number. Although he may have lacked aristocratic ancestry, Young Harvey in every other way answered G.M. Young's description of a typical heir of a late 18th-century aristocrat: 'The son will be a county member too, but he will, in speech and attire conform to the standards of his more refined age, and will debate the Corn Laws on the principles of Ricardo, or lecture to his tenants on Leiebig's Agricultural Chemistry ... the country gentleman of the 19th century is an administrative and scientific man.'[6]

One of Young Harvey's neighbours in Cobham was John Southey, 15th Lord Somerville, one of the country's leading pioneer agriculturists. He kept a famous flock of merino sheep at Fairmile Farm and exchanged ideas with another famous sheep breeder, 'Farmer' George III. Harvey Combe senior had corresponded with Somerville in 1809 concerning this activity and the estate archives contain a list of rams for hire and the cost, signed by Somerville.[7] Towards the end of the previous century Cobham had also been home to Thomas Ruggles who shared his advanced views on farming and conservation of the countryside with his friend Arthur Young, the traveller and writer. Young's 'Annals of Agriculture' were an important source for disseminating the latest ideas on farm management. Another of Young Harvey's neighbours was William Duckett of Weylands Farm at Hersham. Duckett, inventor of a new type of drill plough, also farmed land on Cobham's Fairmile. Although Young Harvey retained his father's flocks he also developed a special interest in cattle breeding and became well known for his herd of short-horns. The estate archives contain 60 catalogues of livestock sales around the country including one at Cobham in 1850. When Young Harvey died the sale of his herd of short-horns raised over £5,000.

In 1822 Young Harvey instructed the Cobham land agent Thomas Crawter to prepare a complete terrier of his Cobham estate.[8] This important document is accompanied by plans both of the whole estate and its various component parts and provides a unique picture of Cobham Park at this time. The estate archives also contain an interesting volume of farm accounts covering the period 1820 to 1823 which provides an important insight into farm management at this period.[9] Many of the entries are in the hand of Bailiff Elsdon and it is almost possible to hear his accent through the phonetic spellings used in many of the entries. It is clear that the farm was being run using all the latest technology and in 1820 there is an entry relating to the sum of £1 16s.3d. paid to Francis for 'menden thrashing machine'. Other farm equipment and vehicles required regular maintenance: in 1821 Worsfold was paid £2 5s.3½d. for 'Grees for Waggons & Carts.' Later that year a payment of 1s 6d was made to Dunford 'for Menden the Heidge'. 'Ditchen' was another regular job as was the 'thetchen' of the various farm buildings such as the 'Colt Boxes at the Dog Kennel'. Local tradesmen continued to be used for specialist work such as 'Shires the Blacksmith', 'Walker the Coller Macker', 'Rokers the Weelrite', 'Peto the Miller', 'Tickner the Carpenter' and 'Parker', who was the local builder 'for Menden Windows at farm & New Barn & Banks & Dogkennel'.

The accounts also contain frequent references to the costs of travelling to and from the local markets at Guildford, Dorking, Ewell and elsewhere and the tolls that had to be paid for using the newly turnpiked roads. In 1820 a total of 12s. 8d. was paid for passing through the 'Ockham Gate' on 19 occasions when coal was being delivered.

Through the farm accounts it is possible to follow the daily life of the farm with its annual cycle of ploughing, sowing and harvesting. The soil needed continual attention to improve crop production and the sheep were used to manure the land. Lime was used to neutralise soil acidity and the accounts contain numerous references to the production of lime probably in one of the kilns that stood at the southern end of the estate near the parish boundary with Horsley and Effingham. Once the lime had been burned it needed to be spread and we read of a payment to 'Woods for spreading 5 kilns of lime at 5s' each. 'Wimen' were used for the more menial tasks on the estate such as 'picken of … stons at 8d a loade' and Mrs Woods who was paid 10d. for 'Turnip picken'. Other casual labour included 'Mole ketchen' which was usually undertaken by 'Arthur'.

Help from outside was needed when the time came to bring in the harvest. The accounts reveal the employment of gangs such as the 'Horsley Men', the 'Farnham Men' and the 'Hamshier Men'. G.E. Mingay has written how many farmers had to resort to the use of 'gangmasters' who recruited bands of workers to work on contract.[10] The work was often excessively arduous but it was not so much the physical strains imposed by gang labour that troubled observers, rather the moral dangers to which young people were exposed when constantly in the company of adults of 'intemperant habits, doubtful morals and foul speech'. It is likely that a group of buildings that formerly stood on the corner of Plough Lane, close to the *Plough Inn*, called 'The Rookery' in the parish rate books, used for housing these migrant workers. In addition to the gangs, women and tramps were also paid to help with the 'harvesten'. Once the harvest was safely in all those who had taken part were treated to the traditional harvest supper. In 1820 George Lynn, one of Cobham's butchers, provided 54lbs of 'beaf' for the harvest supper. 2s. 1d. was spent on bread, 3s. on 'Tabackco' and 1s. for the pipes in which to smoke it.

As in the time of Harvey senior, filling the ice house continued to be an opportunity to celebrate and, in 1821, the sum of 15s. 8d. was paid for 'Bread & Chees for the Men fillen the Ice house'. Beer was provided at a cost of £1.10s. Beer was also provided on other thirst-making occasions such as 'for the Men … when they was at Worke in Bridge Meadowe & unladen Ashes'.

Outside labour was also used for the sheep sheerings and in 1821 'Anscombe & Comp.' were paid £1 11s.3d. for 'Washen & Shearing of 125 sheep'. Again, beer was always provided for the shearers. Local lads were employed on a casual basis to care for the sheep and one entry refers to the sum of 8s. paid to 'the Boye looken after the sheep at Slifful in Turnips'. This was an excellent way of feeding the sheep and manuring the land. The wool produced by the sheep was also sold locally and there is an entry for turnpike tolls when wool was taken to Godalming, a place famous for the manufacture of woollen goods.

Some livestock was sent to London and other markets for sale and this involved the added expense of getting them to their destination. In 1822 Woods was given 2s. for 'Driven the sheep to Ewell and from'. Other livestock was sold locally either at 'Cobham fare' or to local butchers, such as George Lynn whose shop and slaughter house was at Street Cobham on the site of 'The Chancery' and William Elphick whose premises were in Church Street, in the house now called 'Mole Cottage'.

The agricultural unrest of the 1820s and '30s has already been mentioned. Many of those facing unemployment and starvation chose to work outside the law. Poaching was a major problem faced by the landowners and one occurrence of this at Cobham Park in 1838 resulted in the death of Thomas Chipps, one of young Harvey's gamekeepers. Chipps and his fellow keeper James Parker had been attacked by a band of poachers from Kingston led by Thomas Sakers. The death of Chipps caused an uproar in the locality and the *Times* newspaper reported that 'the neighbourhood of Cobham was, from an early hour of the morning, much crowded by persons from Guildford, Ripley, Stoke and the surrounding places, anxious to hear the result of the Coroner's Inquest'. Sakers was eventually apprehended and tried. The jury returned a verdict of manslaughter and Sakers was ordered to be 'transported beyond the seas for the term of his natural life'.[11]

Although Young Harvey worked to make the farm economically viable, the accounts for the period 1819 to 1822 reveal that it was run at a loss during that period. This reflected a period of national depression. In 1819/1820 the total loss was a little over £1,000. The following year it had doubled to a little over £2,000. In 1821/1822 the loss fell again to a little over £1,000. However, in 1822/23 the loss was reduced to just over £400. Progressive agriculture was unlikely to bring returns as high as investment in funds or new commercial enterprises and Thomas Coke's daughter considered farming to be 'a most expensive amusement'.

Despite the pressures and demands of life on the farm, time was made to celebrate national events. In February 1840 estate workers, neighbours and friends were invited to Downside Farm to celebrate 'The Marriage of Our Beloved Queen with Prince Albert of Saxe Gotha'.

On the estate Young Harvey demonstrated his enthusiasm for the new ideas in a flourish of building activity in the 1840s. His new 'model kennels' were important enough to be reproduced as an engraving in 1841.[12] Interest in farm building reached a new height with the Royal Agricultural Society's farm prize competition of 1850 and this may have led Young Harvey to develop Down Farm as a model farm.[13] The architect of the farm is not known and Young Harvey himself may well have designed it. There were certainly plenty of illustrations available of what could be, and was being, done. Down Farm is similar in layout and design to a farm at Stoke Bruerne in Northamptonshire created for the Duke of Grafton by his agent John Gardner in the 1840s.[14] Grafton remodelled a number of his farm buildings at this time and Young Harvey may have known of them through his hunting in that part of the country. Immediately opposite the entrance to Cobham Park house was the site of 'The Old Garden House' which had been purchased by Harvey Combe senior. Young Harvey purchased the land surrounding this property and built an impressive large walled kitchen garden with greenhouses, hot houses and other offices. From the size of this complex and the large range of buildings it is clear that this was also built with more in mind than simply feeding the occupants of Cobham Park, especially taking into consideration the fact that Young Harvey did not have a family to feed. In addition to the model farm and walled kitchen garden, he completely rebuilt the stable block adjoining the mansion. Here he built on the grand scale and provided room for six carriages. The keystone to the arch over the access to the stable yard carries the inscription 'Wood Yard Brewhouse 1849' as if to be a permanent reminder both of his roots and the source of his wealth for both himself and those visiting the estate. In the 1850s Caird described farming in Surrey as being amongst some of the most backward in England, with a lack of capital being invested by landlord and tenant alike. If this is to be believed, then perhaps Young Harvey was striving to set an example of what could be done with the right vision and capital investment.[15]

In 1819 Young Harvey entered into an exchange of land with Thomas Mellor who then owned Downside Mill. This resulted in Harvey acquiring the house that had been built by Alexander Raby at the end of the previous century. The property was then described as 'the messuage or mansion house situate near the River Mole in the parish of Cobham together with the stabling offices and outbuildings thereunto belonging or used therewith with the lawn and pleasure grounds thereunto belonging'.[16] Raby's house was immediately demolished and the site returned to agricultural land. This is somewhat surprising given the high status of the house and its ancillary buildings. Presumably Young Harvey had no need for this additional accommodation and its upkeep and maintenance would have been an unnecessary financial burden on the estate.

Between 1823 and 1845 Young Harvey pursued a rigorous policy of purchasing neighbouring properties as they became available. Hill House in neighbouring Little Bookham was purchased in 1824[17] and in 1828 the substantial property known as Park Farm House was added to the estate.[18] This last property is an important late 16th- or early 17th-century timber-framed house and it was used as the home for the farm bailiff. Close to Park Farm House stood the *Waggon and Horses* ale house which young Harvey purchased in 1835 and demolished to make room for new stables and a stud farm.[19] In 1845 Young Harvey purchased the former rectory which stood next to St Andrew's church. He demolished this building and replaced it with a charming cottage in the 'Gothick' style, now called Rose Lodge.[20] In the same year Chasemore Farm at Downside was added to the estate, thereby linking the properties in the Bookhams and Effingham to the Cobham estate.[21] Chasemore Farm takes its name from the Chasemore family who lived there in the 18th century. Before that it was known as Dudwicks, a name which can be traced back into the medieval period. Further lands in Little and Great Bookham and Effingham were added to the estate between 1847 and 1856.[22] The end result of these various land and property purchases was a much more cohesive and manageable working estate.

The 1820s saw much pressure for new and better housing for the working classes. Increasing numbers of homes in the countryside were being occupied by people who were not working on the land. The housing situation varied greatly from village to village. In areas where a few major landowners held the land, the proprietors might follow a policy of strict control over new building and over the letting of existing cottages. This was partly to reduce the possibility of the occupants becoming claimants for poor relief and an additional burden on the parish rates. In areas that have been termed 'landlord villages' the cottages were likely to be better maintained and better built in the first place. To provide the labouring class with 'the means of greater cleanliness, health, and comfort, in their own homes, extend education, and thus raise the social and moral habits of these most valuable members of the community' was deemed to be 'among the finest pleasures of every landlord'. Although Cobham was not strictly a 'landlord village', those living on the Cobham Park estate probably fared better than many of their fellow villagers. During his ownership of Cobham Park, Young Harvey purchased most of the properties along the east side of Downside Common. These comprised various old cottages and farmhouses which he demolished and replaced with roomy and 'well appointed' workers' cottages. As a result Downside took on much of its present-day appearance with the distinctive cottages on the east side of the common between Elm Tree Cottage and Bookham Common Road having been built as a result. The first two new houses were built in 1855 by George Wood, the Cobham builder, at a total cost of £411 19s.[23] These were probably the houses now known as 'New Cottages'. Young Harvey planned more cottages but it was left to his sister to have them built. In 1859 six cottages were built overlooking Downside Common at the total cost of £1,396 2s.7d. The builder's account also refers to building a Bake House and it may be this building which is now St Matthew's Chapel. The year before he died Young Harvey had arranged for the supply of fresh water for the people of Downside. It was piped from the higher land at Kelseys on the edge of Bookham Common to a pump which still stands outside St Matthew's Chapel. The total cost of the exercise was £1061 13s.3d.

It was not only the provision of good housing and clean water for those employed upon his estate that concerned Young Harvey. Unlike previous owners of the estate he was involved in the affairs of the wider community through the Vestry meeting. The Vestry was the equivalent of the local parish council and one of its most important areas of concern was that of the poor. The 1834 Poor Law Amendment Act resulted in the creation of new Union Workhouses which took people away from their own parish. Before this time each local Vestry dealt with the care of the poor within its own parish. The 1820s were a particularly difficult time because of the depression and unemployment which followed the end of the war with France. The numbers requiring parish assistance increased and in 1822 the Cobham Vestry held a meeting to discuss the 'proprietary of building cottages for the use of paupers'. The parish already had a work house on the Upper Tilt and adjoining this there were several one-room parish cottages for needy cases. However, the income from the parish rate was not sufficient to cover the additional expense of new cottages and the Vestry decided to take advantage of a recently passed Act of Parliament which allowed local vestries to borrow money for such emergencies. On 12 December 1822 the Vestry recorded its decision to accept the offer from young Harvey to advance a sum of £500 for this purpose.[24]

A common aim for those who aspired to the landed gentry in the 19th century was to withdraw from an active business life. F.M.L. Thompson writes that 'even in brewing, the most gentlemanly and least demanding of all businesses, attention to affairs might interfere with the full enjoyment of country life'. However, it is clear that in order to finance the development of the Cobham estate Young Harvey remained firmly involved in the family business. Thompson continues, 'Even though the founder of a fortune might purchase a country place to celebrate his success, his sons were likely to have been born at an early stage in his rise, to have been brought up in the old house in an atmosphere of daily contact with the affairs of the business, and to have been educated in the way that a plain and rising businessman could afford. Thus although a son might inherit a country estate the formative experiences of his youth might well dispose him to take a continuing interest in his father's firm. The grandsons, the third generation, would be the first to be born and brought up in the country seat, the first to be educated as gentlemen's sons, and were thus most likely to be the first to prefer conventional gentlemen's lives for themselves.' And so it was in the Combe family. Young Harvey had grown up with the brewery and had a deep sense of loyalty to the family business. However, it is also clear that in order to finance the development of the Cobham estate he would have to look to the brewery and other sources of income to ensure its sustainability.

Young Harvey was not a man to miss a business opportunity and, in 1824, he speculated by purchasing four shares of £100 each in the newly formed Kensington Canal Company.[25] In 1839 young Harvey and his partners Joseph and William Delafield enlarged the Wood Yard Brewery by spreading across Langley Street and taking in the site that Richard Meaux had set up as a brewery eighty years earlier. Sadly just as a young partner had proved an embarrassment to his father, so Young Harvey was to be embarrassed by the actions of a younger member of the Delafield family. Joseph Delafield died in 1843 leaving his brother as the sole representative of that family. That same year two new partners, Daniel Hale Webb and John William Spicer, were admitted to the business and it was provided that, should Joseph's son Edward wish to become a partner when he came of age, it could be arranged. This Edward decided to do. However, no sooner had he been admitted than he started to draw on the capital which had been invested for him. His partners' worst fears were realised when young Edward eventually withdrew all his capital, and like many another rich man, the theatre or rather the opera became his downfall. Edward Delafield used his capital to finance the Covent Garden Opera House and it was he who laid the foundations of its subsequent musical reputation.

In 1848 Young Harvey and his partners found that the brewery had something else to offer the needs of Londoners in addition to liquid refreshment. This was the year of revolutions across Europe and the Chartists planned to hold a large demonstration in London. Physical force was expected and the Duke of Wellington stationed troops at every danger point, but this was not enough. On the day of the rally 170,000 special constables kept the peace and among them were 150 men from Combe's Brewery. A few days later, the *Morning Advertiser* reported that 'Messrs

Combe and Delafield, the brewers of Long Acre, have ordered a substantial supper to be given this evening at eight o'clock to the whole of the men employed upon their premises, 150 in number, for their excellent conduct on Monday last, having been sworn in as special constables.' [26]

In 1852 Daniel Webb died and new partners joined Combe, Delafield & Co. They were Joseph Bonsor and John Samuel Tanqueray, but still the majority shareholding remained with young Harvey. When Young Harvey died no other member of his family was actively concerned in the brewery or had shown any inclination to be so. Young Harvey's share in it was divided between two nephews, half-brothers, the sons of his youngest brother Charles James Fox Combe. The elder, Richard Henry Combe, had an estate of 1,500 acres at Frensham and was living the life of a country gentleman. The other nephew was Charles Combe who was serving in the army and it was he who was to inherit the Cobham estate.

When Young Harvey made his last will he remembered not only his family but all his servants and employees at the Brewery. Every clerk who had been employed there for at least one year was to receive £50 and every domestic servant at Cobham of at least one year's employment was to receive £10. Additional and more substantial sums were left to the head gardener at Cobham Park and the Coldmans, his faithful butler and cook, were to receive an annuity of £100.

Young Harvey died on 22 November 1858. His sister Mary Anne stayed on at Cobham Park filling her remaining years with good works in her brother's memory. She paid for more new cottages to be built at Downside and made sure that the scheme to provide a supply of fresh water and a pump was successfully completed. However, her most important legacy was the building of a new school on land which she purchased for £4,000 out of her own funds and gave to the diocesan authorities. The school, opened in 1860, was dedicated to her late brother's memory. There was some mild disagreement at first concerning the school because the vicar and churchwardens wanted attendance to be restricted to children who attended the Church of England. However, Mary Anne was insistent that the school should serve all the village children irrespective of churchmanship. It is evident that Mary Anne was of an independent turn of mind for in spending her own money she was determined not to accept any Government grants and therefore no Government interference. The school buildings still stand in Cedar Road as a lasting memorial to Mary Anne and her brother. Although no longer home to the village school, the use of the buildings as a library and adult education centre means that they still serve the community in accordance with the terms of the original grant. Mary Anne Combe died on 6 August 1861 and was laid to rest with her father and brother in the family mausoleum.

12

A New Squire and a New House

Fate smiled kindly upon Charles Combe when, at the age of 25, he inherited both the Cobham Park estate and half his uncle's share in the brewery. In his childhood his prospects must have appeared limited. He was the first son of his father's second marriage, ranking ninth in the family, and was to be followed by six more brothers and sisters. His father was a son of Charles James Fox Combe, the youngest surviving son of Alderman Combe. Charles J.F. Combe had married firstly Henrietta Anne Church, who died in 1834, and then Eliza, daughter of William Roberts of Norwich. The economic pressures of a large family led Charles and Eliza to choose to make their home at Honfleur, Normandy, and their younger children were born and educated in France. It was only in his later life that Charles J.F. returned to England and he died at Stoke D'Abernon in 1875.

Charles, the inheritor of Cobham Park, was born in 1836. On completion of his education he pursued a career in the army and served in the 3rd Bombay Light Cavalry throughout the 1857 Persian war. He took part in a celebrated cavalry charge at Kooshab and this episode was captured in a dramatic painting which now hangs at Cobham Lodge. On his return to India, Charles served with the Central India Field Force under Sir Hugh Rose through the Indian Mutiny and took part in no fewer than 23 engagements. This exemplary military career resulted in Charles Combe receiving two medals and clasps as well as being mentioned in despatches on a number of occasions.

When peace was finally restored in India and the vast dominions of the East India Company were formally transferred to the Crown, Charles Combe retired from the service. It is likely that he was aware of his expected inheritance before his uncle's death, as both his uncle and aunt had taken a close interest in, and developed a strong affection for, their young nephew. They were no doubt impressed by Charles's military career and it is likely that his aunt had purchased his army commission. Charles is said to have borrowed funds from his uncle and aunt to replace the horse that had been shot from under him in the Kooshab episode. Whilst it might have been accepted that the young officer would not have repaid the loan, Charles did pay off the debt, no doubt raising his esteem in the eyes of his uncle and aunt. Mary Anne Combe's willingness to assist her young nephew also extended to her paying the bills for his clothing, uniform and equipment, the receipts for which survive among the family papers.

It is not clear when Charles took up residence at Cobham Park but he was clearly mindful of his debt to his aunt who continued to live at the house until her death in August 1861. After a discreet period of mourning following his aunt's death, Charles married his distant cousin Marianne Harriett Catherine Inglis in November 1861. It might have been expected that Charles would have chosen a bride from a wealthy or aristocratic family but Marianne was the only daughter of Captain Patrick Inglis R.N. of Edinburgh who, according to a story in the family, had been somewhat impoverished by family matters outside his control. Presumably Charles and Marianne chose to wait until Charles came into his inheritance before marrying. Their union produced a large family of nine sons and six daughters.

In addition to the Cobham estate, Charles Combe inherited half his uncle's share in the London brewery. The other half was left to Richard Henry, Charles's elder brother by his father's first marriage, who married Esther Holloway in 1857 and settled at Pierrepoint House, Frensham, Surrey. Following the death of their uncle's partner, William Delafield, the main conduct of the brewery reverted to the Combe family and remained with them until the amalgamation with Watney's and Reid's in 1898.[1]

Between the death of his aunt in 1861 and his own death in 1920 Charles Combe was one of the biggest landowners in the district and, although never lord of the manor, he exercised more influence and control over local affairs during that period than any one else. The manor of Cobham had belonged to the Page family who lived at nearby Pointers but, when Miss Sophia Page died in 1860, she left the manor to her cousin Francis John Mount who lived outside the county.

Charles was keen to follow in his uncle's footsteps and continue to make the Cobham Park estate into an homogenous and self-sufficient unit. In 1866 he purchased Downside Mill for £3,150. The mill and its associated buildings formed an awkward intrusion into the estate, surrounded as it was by the home farm and the park. Corn had probably been milled on this site since the time of Domesday Book and, as already recorded, the buildings were later converted into a paper mill and then used to power Alexander Raby's iron works. When Raby left Cobham Thomas Mellor converted the buildings to a flock mill. Charles Combe turned the mill into a saw yard and workshops to serve the estate. Later a turbine was installed to generate electricity for the house.

Charles Combe was also looking to extend the acreage of his estate and in 1872 he purchased the land opposite Cobham Mill which sits in a large loop of the river. This had formerly belonged to Ham Manor from where it had been farmed in the 18th century. This land is actually an island separated from Cobham Park grounds by a small watercourse that cuts across the loop from opposite the Tilt to just above Downside Bridge, nearly opposite the parish church.[2] Maintenance of cattle and other livestock was clearly an important concern in running the estate. In February 1870 a local newspaper announced the sale of 'Very Superior FAT STOCK' which was to take place at Cobham Park. Included in the sale were '44 short-horn steers and heifers, 27 West Highland runts, 100 4-tooth South-down wethers, and 100 Down tegs, of the finest quality, and in prime condition.'

One of Charles Combe's first public roles in Cobham was to chair a committee which sought to enclose the three hundred or so acres of common land which had been left after the enclosures of the late 18th century. Whilst Combe was able to muster considerable support in Cobham, he was strongly and successfully opposed by the lord of the manor in whom the commons were vested.

Charles and his young wife were planning for the future and soon began to find Cobham Park mansion too small and inconvenient for their needs. Within the estate archives is a rough drawing showing a proposed enlargement of the house.[3] The drawing is not dated but the paper is watermarked 1858. Estate accounts reveal that Charles Combe undertook repairs to the old house shortly after he inherited the property and payments for a new roof are recorded in 1862. By 1869 Charles and Marianne had started a family and there were already three sons. In that same year Charles Combe, as one of the chief promoters for a scheme to bring the railway into Cobham, was called to give evidence before a Select Parliamentary Committee which was considering whether the scheme should be allowed. During questioning one of the committee members commented to Combe, 'Yours is a very nice estate at Cobham and a very convenient mansion house', to which Combe replied, 'It is not a convenient house because I am going to pull it down.' Except for the alterations made by Young Harvey, the house was probably still very much in its 18th-century condition at this time. However, it may not just have been inconvenience that led to this decision. A more modern and grandiose house would have been important to the family's social status.

There is a family story that Cobham Park mansion was damaged by a fire shortly after Charles Combe inherited the estate but no record of it can be found in local newspapers of the time. However what is certain is that in 1870 Charles and Marianne left Cobham Park to take up temporary residence at Fir Grove, Weybridge and, shortly after this, demolition work on the old mansion began.

The long-standing and close historical relationship between land and power meant that land had become the principal symbol of authority. It was probably this aspect of authority rather than the anticipation of significant increments of rent that explains the rise in both the price of rural land and the number of great houses, like Cobham Park, being built or remodelled in the 1870s. Charles Combe chose as his architect Edward Middleton Barry, R.A., son of Sir Charles Barry who had helped design the Palace of Westminster. In addition to completing his father's work at Westminster, Edward Barry's most significant contribution to the London architectural scene is the Royal Opera House in Covent Garden. He also designed the adjacent Floral Hall, which was heavily influenced by the Crystal Palace used for the Great Exhibition of 1851. Cobham Park is one of only two surviving country houses designed by Barry.[4] Barry's original proposal for the new house was rejected. Unfortunately the drawings have not survived. However, the second design was accepted and work was soon underway to demolish the old house. Most of the materials were sold for scrap but some items such as the columns from the front entrance porch have survived. It may also be that a carved consol bracket found recently near Downside Farm came from the old house. The new house was built in the footprint of the former house and the old cellars were retained. The building contractor was the firm of Holland and Hammer who were paid £32,684 15s.3d. for the contract.[5] The building of the new house was marred by the death of two workmen who were killed in a fall from the scaffolding in 1871. They were buried in St Andrew's churchyard where a monument to their memory was placed by Charles Combe.[6]

In the 1960s, when Victorian architecture was unfashionable, the style of the new house was described by the late Professor Pevsner as 'ugly French Renaissance'. It may be that Combe chose the French style to reflect the country where he had spent his formative years. Like most Victorian country houses, Cobham Park was virtually in two separate parts, the main or family block and the service wing. The main block was designed to be conspicuous and elaborate whilst the service wing had to be 'invisible' like the servants themselves, and was hidden by bushes and earth banks. The house had three separate staircases: the grand staircase rising from the entrance hall, a more private staircase for the family, and the third for the servants.

By 1873 the property was ready for occupation. The house had been built to the very latest standards, and when electricity was installed a few years later, it was reputed to be the third in the county to have this new power source. In November 1883 Charles Combe was 'thinking of putting up a water wheel in the back stream in Park Wood and making it pump that nice spring water that is always running to waste into the tank in the Roundabout'. The Suffolk firm of Whitmore and Binyon was engaged to install a small water wheel which still survives. The work was in hand by March of the following year and by June Combe recorded that 'the water wheel was started last week and works capitally.' This also provided a 'capital bathing place' at the Mill head. Alterations and improvements to the house were also in hand and a conservatory was added which made 'a capital place for growing roses and flowers'. Other more mundane work was also being carried out, leading Combe to complain that 'Holland and Hammer are pulling the house to pieces, altering the drainage system; this was perfect, so far as it could be, at the time the house was built, but the system has been completely changed since then, and what was perfect then is all wrong now! … they are making an awful mess.' [7]

When the family took up residence in the new house there were eight children, the youngest, Boyce Haddon, having been born in 1871. Seven more children were to follow and, in 1880, Charles Combe commissioned the sculptor F.J. Williamson to execute marbles statues of several of the children.[8] Williamson lived at nearby Esher and had been honoured with commissions from Queen Victoria. Correspondence between Combe and Williamson reveals that the artist was struggling financially at this time and had to ask his patron for several advances which Combe was reluctant to give.

The new house at Cobham Park was ideal for Combe's expanding family. However, in addition to being a family home it was also the 'big house' for the surrounding neighbourhood. A contemporary publication reported that 'as an extensive landowner,

Mr Combe affords employment to a considerable number of men and their families, who are mostly housed in excellent cottages with good gardens.'9 So it was that Cobham Park became the centre of life in Cobham. In this role he continued his family's philanthropic traditions. In 1899 he provided Cobham's volunteer fire service with a new fire engine. This machine was handed over at a ceremony which took place in the park. The *Cobham Parish Magazine* reported, 'Punctually at three o'clock the various brigades, eight in number, which had been asked to take part in the festivities, filed in consecutively through the Park Gates, and together with and headed by our local brigade formed up in a line along the edge of the lake. As soon as everything was in order Mrs Combe stepped forward and started the new engine on its destined work as a protector of Cobham property by breaking over it a bottle of champagne, whose contents evaporated amid the ringing of plaudits of those present, which were immediately followed by the strains of the National Anthem.' In addition to providing a new fire engine, Charles Combe assisted in the building of Cobham's first village hall and the provision of a public cemetery on the Tilt. The family later helped to provide Cobham with its first Cottage Hospital which was opened by HRH The Duchess of Albany in 1905. In those days before the Welfare State needs within the parish were usually met from various funds to which the better-off subscribed and the name of Combe was nearly always found as one of the largest benefactors.

Charles Combe's involvement in proposals to bring the railway to Cobham has already been mentioned. In 1869 he organised a public meeting at the *White Lion* inn at Street Cobham to assess public support and offered to subscribe £500 towards the scheme. At the Parliamentary Committee the following year, Combe explained that he required between 120 and 130 tons of coal every year for his house, gardens and farm. This had to be brought by barge to Thames Ditton and then carted to Cobham. The railway would prove invaluable for this and for transporting farm produce from Cobham to the markets at Kingston and London. Unfortunately, due to Queen Victoria's intervention, Combe and the people of Cobham had to wait another 14 years for the railway to arrive. One of the Queen's favourite residences was Claremont at nearby Esher and the proposed line would have passed very close to the estate. Another line, proposed in the 1860s, would have brought the railway into the centre of Cobham and then out in a southerly direction between Cobham Court and Pyports. The line would have passed very close to Cobham Park Stud. Combe was not happy with this proposal and both he and his stud manager lodged objections. When the new line to Guildford via Cobham was constructed in 1885 it cut across Combe's land. It is believed that Combe had hoped for a station, or halt, at Downside to serve Cobham Park. In September 1883 he wrote to his eldest son, 'The railway is getting on fast: they are nearly at the Bridge over the river, and are burning clay in the field by the water tank.' The following year he wrote, 'The railway has nearly got through and we shall be very glad when these fellows finish: the Keeper says they have been a very rough lot this last fortnight.' A story in the family says how Charles Combe forbade his daughters to go anywhere near the construction works because of the navvies' colourful language. In December 1883, Ethel Combe had a lucky escape when driving a friend to see the railway. Where the line crossed the track between Down Farm and Muggeridge Wood, the horse shied at some snow, upsetting the cart in which they were sitting. Combe commented, 'It is a very dangerous place and I must make the contractors put up a fence.'

But the house was, of course, primarily a home for the family and their friends. Visitors to the 'big house' included the poet Matthew Arnold who lived at Painshill Cottage at Street Cobham and, in September 1883, Charles Combe wrote to his son telling them that the Arnolds had been dinner guests at Cobham Park just before leaving for a lecture tour of the USA. Another visitor was Rosa Lewis, better known as the 'Duchess of Duke Street', who was a friend of Combe's valet. Charles Combe's sons and daughters had many friends within the local community. One particular family were the Lushingtons who came to live at Pyports, opposite the parish church. Vernon Lushington was the son of Judge Stephen Lushington, a noted barrister who had represented Queen Caroline in her divorce from George IV. Vernon was a great patron of the arts and included among his friends a number of the Pre-Raphaelite circle of painters. It was through Vernon that the young Edward Burne Jones and Dante Gabriel Rossetti met for the first time. Vernon's wife Jane died at an early age. 'She caught cold at one of her 'Barn' entertainments and could not shake it off.'[10] Charles Combe wrote to Vernon Lushington to express his sympathy and went on to say, 'She [Jane Lushington] was a special favourite of ours and one of the few, very few, people my wife cared about.'[11] The three Lushington daughters were quickly 'adopted' by Mrs Leslie Stephen, mother of Virginia Woolf. The young ladies of the Lushington and Combe families were good friends and spent much time together, often playing music. In a diary entry for 3 January 1893, Margaret Lushington describes an evening with the Combe family and concludes with the words 'Funny funny Combes'.[12] An extract from the unpublished diaries of Susan Lushington provides a fascinating word portrait of the Combe family in the 1890s and this is reproduced as Appendix 2.

In the fashion of the day, Charles Combe also kept a London house for the season. This was at 27, Portland Place (now the Swedish Embassy). In May 1884 Charles Combe wrote to his eldest son, 'We are going to give a ball on 5th June (at the London residence) and everything will be upside down for some days; a great nuisance.' A few days later he wrote, 'The ball went off very well, and we had about 300 people, notwithstanding it was a miserable wet night. The flowers were lovely, some 200 pots of scarlet geraniums being tied to the banister, the pots hidden with green; some splendid palms were about the rooms and hall.' The guests were treated to 'an excellent supper' and entertained by 'Liddell's orchestra'. '40 lbs of strawberries and any amount of shawberries in bowls of cream were eaten, and some ten dozen champagne drunk.' At another ball held in June 1891 upwards of 500 guests were entertained in lavish style and 'dancing was kept with great spirit until four o'clock'.[13] In addition to a London house, Charles Combe, a keen sailor, kept a succession of ocean-going yachts. These were moored at Dartmouth and a surviving logbook records journeys to the Mediterranean. Combe's last vessel, the *Dotterel*, was sold in 1908 and later requisitioned for use in the First World War when a torpedo sank her.

In 1885 Charles Combe followed in the footsteps of both his uncle Harvey and his brother Richard and became Sheriff of Surrey. He was not too happy about this and wrote to his son Charles, 'It is rather a nuisance and I believe I could get off, as Uncle Harvey served, and it is unusual in Surrey to tax the property Sheriff two generations running.' As Sheriff Combe was required to act as returning officer of the election held in November of that year. He wrote to his eldest son, 'I have been so busy with these elections that I have not had time to write. Every day somewhere – Today I returned Mr Cubitt with 4621 votes against Mr Harris 2306!'

Family letters from this period are full of little insights into life at Cobham Park and the local community at this time. In an undated letter to his son Charles, Combe wrote, 'We have begun to make a cricket ground in the park – the man from Lords came down and marked it off and is coming again to level it – he says it will be a very good ground. The billiard room will not be finished for another month but will be very nice when done.' From 1883 to 1885 Charles Combe junior travelled the world, visiting the USA, Japan, China and Australia. The letters sent to him by his father usually included a few references to life back home, such as the installing of 'the new eel trap, at the Mills, is nearly done – it was a big job and it will take some big catches to pay for it.' A little later Combe reported, 'There have been a couple of otters in the river lately.' In May 1884 'A very sharp frost of 17 deg has utterly destroyed all the fruit at Cobham and all over the country. There was a wonderful show, the best for many years, but all has been killed.' In 1883 the marriage of the butler was a cause for concern: 'A married butler is rather a nuisance'. The butler Bristow decided to retire the year after his marriage and Combe wrote that he was looking for a new butler; 'a nuisance changing butlers'.

The letters exchanged between the children also contain local news items. In March 1900 Edgar Combe wrote to his brother Edmond describing the highest floods in Cobham for 53 years when 'Charlie caught a fish on the croquet lawn'. At the farm 'the water was a foot high in the cart horse stables & they had to be taken out, the water on one side of the mill (at Downside) & the water on the other joined so that there were no waterfalls.' The water was over two feet high in 'Sweetlove's mill' at Cobham. 'Harvey drove from the station in Evelyn's old cart ... he first got in the water at the fire station & by Sweetlove's it was so deep that it nearly went into the cart.' Charles Combe wrote to Edmond of how people had to use carts to get to church, 'the roads being two feet under water'. In May 1902 Charles Combe wrote to Edmond: 'They say our Cobham drainage is all wrong and won't be ready for another year – Engineers and Contractors blame one another.'

The gardens and parkland required constant attention and in 1904 a 'Ha-ha' was constructed at Cobham Park to improve the view from the front of the house into the park. The work on the 'Ha-ha' received several setbacks due to very heavy frosts. The kitchen gardens produced everything necessary to feed the large family occupying the 'big house' and those who looked after them. A good description of both the grounds of the house and the kitchen garden was printed in *The Gardeners' Chronicle* of 4 February 1905. Among the delicacies then to be found in the kitchen garden were apricots, peaches, nectarines, figs and asparagus. A great variety of seasonal flowers were grown in the plant houses and used for decorating both Cobham Park and the London house.

In addition to rebuilding the family mansion, accepting public office and fulfilling his role in the life of the local community, Charles Combe also continued to enlarge and consolidate his estate at Cobham. He pursued a policy of acquiring neighbouring land and properties as they came onto the market. These were mostly contiguous to the Park, and led to the creation of Cobham Park estate. It was, and is, the Cobham Park estate that moulded and restricted the development of Cobham south of the river Mole, giving it much of the character which it retains to this day. Charles Combe's purchases of Downside Mill and the land opposite Cobham Mill have already been mentioned. In 1884 Elm Farm on Cobham Tilt came on to the market. The farm was part of a much larger estate centred on Ashford Farm on Cobham Tilt, which was put up for sale following the death of its owner Edward Bennett. The purchase of Elm Farm extended the estate to north side of the Mole and provided valuable riverside meadow land ideal for grazing a dairy herd. Further local property acquisitions over the following years included Church Gate House (1896), Faircroft, Between Streets (1897), Tinmans' Row, Downside (1898), cottages at Plough Corner (1902), and Cobham Lodge (1905). Building work on the existing estate included a new laundry and laundry cottage (1884), Emlyn Lodge near Downside Mill, Keeper's Cottage and kennels overlooking Downside Common and, in the early years of the 20th century, Korea Cottages on the Upper Tilt, which were built on land that had formerly belonged to the parish workhouse.

One of Charles Combe's special interests was the breeding of racehorses and he developed the Stud Farm, which had been started by his uncle, into a thriving commercial enterprise. The fortunes of the Stud were built on a famous stallion called Blair Athol, 'the Blaze-faced King of Cobham', which was purchased for £13,000. In the course of his life this horse sired no fewer than 60 yearlings, and in the 1896 Derby five of the runners were his progeny. In that same year the *Cobham Parish Magazine* reported that the annual sale of yearlings at the Stud meant 'a special train down from town for the occasion, and this was fairly well filled but apparently most of the travellers went in for the inspection and free lunch rather than for the business in as much as there were very few purchasers.' According to the autobiography of William Allison, the Stud manager, this particular sale brought to Cobham HRH The Prince of Wales, later Edward VII, accompanied by his mistress Lillie Langtry.

In 1900 tragedy struck when Marianne Combe died and the family and estate were plunged into mourning. On 10 February Charles Combe wrote to his son Edmond who was then away in the navy informing him, 'Your Mother is dangerously ill with scarlet fever – with two nurses looking after her'. Two days later Combe had to write again to Edmond. 'You will be very grieved to hear that your dear Mother died last night. She caught Scarlet fever (we think at Portsmouth) and yesterday it took a sudden turn for the worse – and she passed away peacefully at 10 last night.' The widowed Charles was grief stricken. On 24 March Edgar Combe wrote to his brother Edmond, 'It was awful about mother, so sudden, I did not know she was ill. Pa they say was awful crying, hair all on end, hat on the back of head, he bursts out crying now sometimes & is always sighing, they have cleared up all Ma's things drawers & drawers full of letters, cupboards full of old dresses, crinolines etc. in one case they found a whole drawer of receipts & at the very back Dorothy's bridesmaid present from Percy, they found bank notes for 10£ & 20£ lost in old letters diamonds rings in various odd places etc. sunshades & umbrellas by the ton enough to supply all the servants & a lot over.'

Despite his deep genuine grief at losing his wife, it was not that long afterwards when, much to his family's disapproval, Charles Combe developed a close friendship with his neighbour, Mrs Alice Ethel Cushney of Painshill, who was then still married. In February 1903 Edgar Combe wrote to his brother Edmund about the reaction of their sister Florence to her father's visits to Painshill. 'She looks on it in a sort of religious light and says it is very wrong of him to go up there & all that sort of thing.' Combe told his daughter that if she wished to continue to live at Cobham she must be civil to Mrs Cushney. Dorothy Combe wrote: 'If only he knew how much people talked about him and Mrs C & the people said that we treated him badly so he went up to Pains Hill, he would know how hard it was to be civil to her ... Percy is furious & won't come near the place again, and all this fuss is about a woman who is married.'

Alexander Cushney died on 3 July 1903 and Charles Combe wrote to his son Edmund the following day: 'Mr Cushney died rather suddenly yesterday morning, tho' he had been rather bad the last week.' Three years later, in 1906, the widow became the second Mrs Combe. It is said that Mrs Cushney made it a condition of her acceptance of Combe's proposal of marriage that he should purchase the Painshill estate from her late husband's executors. This he did and, following his marriage to Mrs Cushney, Combe decided to leave Cobham Park and make Painshill, which had been modernised and enlarged by Richard Norman Shaw, his principal residence. Cobham Park then became the home of his eldest son Charles. In the same year as Charles Combe purchased Painshill, he also bought two fields at Street Cobham, one of which later became the home of Cobham Cricket Club. Two other acquisitions in this year were Bridge Meadow, between Church Gate House and Downside Bridge (formerly a part of Little Bridge Green), and further land at Cobham Tilt known as Hook Meadow, Osier Meadow and Steward's Mead.

In 1905 Cobham's old manor house, Cobham Court, came on the market following the death of T.J. Bennett, who had inherited the property from his brother in 1900. Combe entered into negotiations with Bennett's sister and eventually added this valuable property to his portfolio. In addition to Cobham Court and its farm, Combe also purchased the Hamwell Meadows which lay next to the river, between the farm and the Leg O'Mutton Field. It is said that 'Hamwell' became corrupted to 'Anvil' in the 19th century when a surveyor from the Ordnance Survey wrote down the name after a conversation with one of the locals who must have spoken with a rich country accent and dropped his aitches. As if Cobham Park, Painshill and Cobham Court were not enough, Combe took the opportunity, also in 1905, to purchase Cobham Lodge and Cossins Farm, which had been sold out of the estate in Carhampton's time. Following the completion of these purchases, Combe now owned a great swathe of land and properties stretching from Painshill in the north west to Down Farm in the south east. The only other purchases made by Combe before his death were 'Holly Cottages' and an old neighbouring cottage at Downside. The old cottage was subsequently demolished and replaced by 'New Cottages'.

In 1914 the country was plunged into what became known as the Great War. The Combe family, like so many others, were directly affected when Kenneth, Charles' third son, was killed in action in France in 1914, and his seventh son, Herbert, enlisted in the Hussars and distinguished himself by receiving the DSO with bar. After Charles Combe's move to Painshill, his daughter Dorothy remained at Cobham Park to housekeep for her brother Charles. Another son, Edmund, originally destined for the navy, returned from South America and enlisted. Dorothy's letters to Edmund provide glimpses into life at 'the big house' during those difficult years. Staffing was a major problem and in April 1918, when the Government brought in a bill to call up men between the ages of 40 and 51, she wrote, 'We may lose Poulter (48) here, all the other men are over 51. The bad war news helps recruiting – people flock to the offices on those occasions – as long as we hold the brutes it is something.' In a letter written in September 1918 from Cobham Park, Dorothy wrote that she was planning to go to London: 'I feel I must get away from housekeeping for a bit, it will also save the coal & jam besides which several of the maids have given notice to go and do munition work – we shall be able to come down when we like as we are leaving the old cook, and the comfortable head-housemaid ... We have got in all the coal we can, but it will not be sufficient to keep the kitchen fire going! We shall have a wood fire upstairs & the servants will have one wood fire to sit by downstairs. Central heating will be out of the question, so the house will be rather like a barn!' Staff at the farm were also being taken away including the cowman, the shepherd and the stockman.

Dorothy's 'war effort' was not just confined to housekeeping. She helped at the local temporary hospital at Heywood (now the International Community School). In April 1918 she wrote to Edmund, 'Just off to the hospital, we are filling up there. 15 men straight from the front came in last Monday much to the V.A.Ws. delight. If ever you are wounded be sure & try and get to Heywood! You couldn't do better. Mrs Butler tries to make it as little like a hospital and as much like a house as possible for the men.' A letter to Edmund from his father dated February 1918 refers to the rationing caused by the war: 'We have no motor now, not allowed any petrol – a great nuisance and horses are not allowed oats ... Everybody is on very limited rations from today – nobody has anything to spare.' To add to their misery the weather turned very bad with snow, rain and wind. 'The whole country is under water, the road to the Station is blocked – the river being up to the wall of the White house!'[14] By June, Combe wrote, 'There is hardly a man left in Cobham, and one can't get anything done.'

When peace eventually came in 1918, Combe wrote to Edmond, 'There was not much done in Cobham by way of Peace Celebrations, but a Committee have issued an 'idea' of what they think of doing later on. The tradesmen and village folks would like it carried out, but the money will be the difficulty. They won't subscribe much, while the 'rich' are not in favour of processions, sports, open air dancing, costume cricket matches, Flares – much better buy Victory Bonds, and so clear off some of our Huge Debt.'

One of Charles Combe's last letters was a note dated 23 May 1920 to his son Charles concerning a right of way over the railway at Downside Farm. He finished the letter with, 'Got spectacles at last but am not to do much … this is my first letter!' In August 1920 the vicar of Cobham wrote in the *Parish Magazine* of the community's shock at the loss of the parish's 'leading layman and … one of its best friends'. The vicar went on to describe Charles Combe as 'a model Squire' who had a 'love of justice and square dealing, hatred of humbug, contempt for empty show and for anything even verging on 'swagger' or 'side'.'

Between the death of his aunt in 1861 and his own death in 1920 Charles Combe, landowner and a director of one of the largest breweries in the country, 'reigned' as a beneficent squire of Cobham. During those 60 years Cobham Park became firmly established as Cobham's 'big house'. Combe had lived through a difficult period for the landed gentry. The agricultural decline from the 1870s onwards was followed by heavy taxation, and the war brought further problems with the loss of manpower to work the land and run the estate. Despite all this Charles Combe managed to maintain and even enlarge the Cobham Park estate. His passing brought to an end an autocratic but beneficent rule of a large part of Cobham. Charles Combe had been very much a product of the Victorian age and, after his passing, life at Cobham Park, on the estate, and in the wider community, would never be the same.

13

THE ENDING OF THE OLD ORDER

When Charles Combe died in 1920 his son, Charles Harvey, who was then 57 years old, succeeded him. Like the late King Edward VII, Charles Harvey's time had seemed long in coming, even though he had assumed control of Cobham Park when his father remarried and moved to Painshill. The death of the old squire marked a dramatic watershed in the history and fortunes of Cobham Park, coming as it did less than two years after the ending of the 'war to end all wars'. That event was to have an enormous impact on the economic and social make up of the country. The war had robbed the country of a generation of young men. Women had been 'emancipated' by the role they took in the war effort, working in factories and developing an independent life style. It was clear that life could never be the same and what was happening nationally eventually touched every community that made up the land. The post-war generation began to question and react against what they saw as the restrictive order and institutions developed by their Victorian forebears. It was a case of 'out with the old and in with the new.' The old established social order began to crumble. Soldiers returned from the war having experienced all its horrors, their eyes opened by foreign travel. They needed jobs and houses. No longer would it be easy to run large country estates near London such as Cobham Park. Cities and towns were expanding; old estates were being broken up and sold for development. There was a move away from the land as men, and women, sought employment in the towns.

This ending of the old order was soon being felt in places like Cobham. Charles Harvey Combe had already been spending a large amount of his time away from Cobham. In addition to a London apartment in Jermyn Street, in the 1890s, and in a further attempt to establish his own independence, Charles Harvey had purchased an estate called The Grange at Bonchurch, Isle of Wight, and chose to spend much of his time there. He was very keen on gardening and the island provided the perfect climate for indulging in this particular passion. The estate at Cobham was being run by a partially absent landlord and much of its administration was left in the hands of others such as Captain P. Ellis, a soldier invalided in the war, who was employed by Combe as his secretary in 1920. Ellis, with his wife, moved into Emlyn Lodge near Downside Farm and set up his office in the schoolroom at the big house. In that same year Strutt & Parker, who continue to manage the Cobham Park estate, first took up that role.

Cobham Park had been the creation of Charles Combe senior and his son seemed not to hold any particular sentimental attachment to it; he had only known the old mansion as a small boy. Charles Combe senior had built his house for his large family. When Charles Harvey inherited he had no wife, let alone a family, and the mansion must have seemed like some gigantic white elephant. Just one year after his father's death Charles Harvey was expressing his fears for the changes in the appearance of the district and this led him to consider selling the estate. In June 1921 he wrote to his Agent: 'I have begun to realise that the district is rapidly losing its agricultural character and becoming a suburban and residential area; this change will be hastened by the coming of the London 'bus' and half hourly service of electric trains with their crowds of small house tenants.'[1] By 1925 Combe was beginning to consider selling up at least part of the estate for development. Hampton & Son undertook a survey of the estate south of the Mole. The area in question comprised some 925 acres. The advice was that the estate might not sell as a whole and that it would be preferable to divide it into lots and then sell by auction. A suggestion had been made that Combe might wish to develop some of the land himself and, with this in mind, land next to Elm Farm on the Tilt was considered. However Strutt and Parker reminded Combe that there was a problem inasmuch as 'the Parish Road is not made up beyond the Cemetery'. The road beyond, leading past Korea Cottages, was still an unmade track across the common. In July 1925 his friend George Trollope wrote to Combe: 'I cannot help thinking that you are unduly pessimistic about the future of Cobham Park ... I feel that the proposals in the Town Planning Scheme have saved the parish from evils which have befallen other adjoining parishes, owing to this neglect of similar actions, for many years to come. The Rural District Council is a much more important and efficient body than I supposed before I joined them & I should say there is a very remote chance of their being absorbed in a larger body for some time to come.' Any further thoughts on selling up or development were shelved – at least for the time being.

Despite Trollope's assurances, Combe remained gloomy about the future of Cobham and in December 1925 he wrote to the tenant of Cobham Court: 'Cobham is bound to develop as London spreads, and the Town Planning scheme is attempting to prevent any such disaster as has befallen Fetcham and Bookham. For the sake of the neighbourhood I can only hope that the houses will be of a decent character ... I have long foreseen that we are rapidly becoming a purely residential neighbourhood and farms of secondary importance.' At the start of the following year Combe wrote again to the same tenant, 'I have no faith whatsoever under existing circumstances in the future of farming'. Despite a temporary reprieve during the Second World War II, Combe's statement has proved to be sadly prophetic.

In July 1922 Charles H. Combe married Dorothy Mabel Livingstone. Dorothy had qualified as a nurse during the First World War. She was a physiotherapist and masseuse. When Charles's unmarried sister, another Dorothy, developed rheumatoid arthritis, Dorothy Livingstone came down to Cobham from The Star and Garter Home at Richmond to help treat her. The treatment included Dorothy Combe and her nurse being taken to a spa in France and, in what the family called 'true Combe fashion', Thomas Cook was contacted to arrange the visit that entailed the hire of a complete railway carriage. By the end of the treatment Charles realised that he had fallen in love with the young nurse and proposed marriage. At first Dorothy was shocked and took herself off to Wales to consider the proposal. However, having consulted her mother, she later returned and the two were married. In 1924 twin daughters, Anne and Rosemary, were born.[2] Two years after that, in 1926, a son, Charles Harvey Christian Combe, was born at Cobham, thereby providing a successor to the estate.

Between the births of the twins and their only son, Charles and Dorothy Combe's routine of orderly life at Cobham Park was temporarily shattered when their butler, Duncan McKenzie, killed himself using his master's revolver. A coroner's inquest, held at the *Running Mare* on Cobham Tilt, heard that McKenzie had been a man of 'nervous temperament' and was worried about his invalid son. The jury returned a verdict of 'suicide whilst of unsound mind'.

Having served as MP for the Chertsey Division of Surrey between 1892 and 1907, Combe took up another office in 1929 when, like his father and great uncle, he became High Sheriff of the County.

Although he chose to spend a considerable amount of his time at The Grange, Combe did not neglect the Cobham estate. In 1921 he renewed his insurance policy for his staff which then consisted of '13 indoor servants, 2 Gardeners, 1 Gamekeeper, 1 Laundryman, 1 Carpenter, 1 Painter, 1 Basement Porter, 1 Valet who loads and Casual Labourers.'[3] Only two property purchases were made during Charles Harvey's ownership of the estate. Both were made in 1925. Elm Tree Cottage overlooking Downside Common was purchased from the Jetten family and Cobham Mill from A.H. Moore.

Combe had surprisingly advanced views on conservation and country matters which emanated from practical considerations rather than from tradition or sentimentality. In September 1926 he wrote to the Master of one hunt, 'I have no foxes. When proper foxhounds ceased to meet in this neighbourhood, I had the foxes destroyed & shall continue to do this. I must say I did not regret this decision, what with live electric wire on the rails, and the general urbanisation of the district, I am not surprised at it. The appalling crowds of so called sportsmen were a welcome disappearance, open gates, smashed fences & crops ridden over make me only too glad to see the last of them.' Three years later he wrote to another Hunt Master, 'I am anxious to preserve as far as I can the rapidly diminishing flora & fauna of the district, one or two otters have been seen but I should be glad if you can whip off hounds before they enter my property. I am afraid I have very little sympathy with the destruction of these animals. There are very few left.'

The matter of a Cobham Town Planning Scheme raised its head again in 1931. A proposal was made for a road across Mill Mead (opposite Cobham Mill) and through Rose Lodge Wood to Downside Bridge. His agents advised Combe that he would probably be able to oppose it successfully. It was agreed that the construction of any these new roads should not be undertaken 'without the written consent of the owner of Cobham Park; or that the house should cease to be used as a private dwellinghouse; or that the estate or a substantial part of it shall been developed.' However, despite these assurances Combe continued to be concerned for the future and in 1935 again considered putting the estate on the market. A letter from the estate solicitors, Stileman Neate & Topping, dated 23 February refers to this.

> I think that you are taking the right view in deciding to get rid of the Cobham Park estate if a satisfactory price can be obtained; though I imagine it will be a bit of a wrench to you. But Cobham is changing so rapidly and really one hesitates to think what the country right down to Woking will be like in ten years time. The development around Byfleet is simply atrocious and I think that from Woking to Waterloo will be a maze of tiny houses within 15 years.

However, at the time of this letter, Combe had only a few months left to live and after that the threat of war put any further plans for sale or development on hold.

In the September 1935 edition of *Cobham Parish Magazine* the vicar wrote, 'The whole Village was deeply shocked to hear of the sudden death of the head of its social community Mr C.H. Combe. He was spending the summer months, according to his custom, with his family in the Isle of Wight. He was taken ill about tea-time, and in spite of every endeavour to restore him, he passed away quietly that evening.' The vicar went on to describe Combe as a man of simple tastes who disliked all ostentation, and who 'avoided the limelight of publicity as much as he could ... He took a lively interest in all local affairs without interfering with any. There is hardly a club, society or organisation in the Village but what has received his support.'

Charles Harvey Combe was succeeded by his only son Charles Harvey Christian Combe who was born at Cobham Park in 1926. He was educated at Eton and served with the R.A. from 1945-7. He married Elizabeth Anne Shiers Lowe, the daughter of Colonel H.D. Lowe of Cobham in 1950.

During the Second World War, Cobham Park was acquired by the Eagle Star Insurance Company when its offices were moved out of London to avoid the bombing. The Eagle Star also occupied several other houses in Cobham including Cedar House.

Charles and Elizabeth Combe moved to Cobham Lodge which was a more conveniently sized house. In 1961 they decided to leave Cobham and moved to Boveridge Park, Dorset, where they lived until 1970. Dominic Charles Harvey, their son, was born in 1955 and, the following year, their daughter Charlotte Marianne Frances was born. Whilst they were living in Dorset, a Strutt & Parker agent, Mr D. Findlay, managed the Cobham Park estate. On Mr Findlay's retirement, the estate continued to be managed by Strutt & Parker.

During the time that Charles and Elizabeth Combe lived away from Cobham the estate went through a difficult time. In 1970 Charles and Elizabeth Combe separated. Charles Combe eventually returned to Cobham and took up residence at Cobham

Court. When the Eagle Star gave up its occupancy of Cobham Park mansion after the war, the house remained empty for several years until it was leased to Alan Grant & Partners. Later, the house was leased by Logica who eventually purchased both the house and the immediate surrounding land. Logica undertook a major restoration of the house but when the company later underwent a major reorganisation of its offices, the house was sold to Beechcroft who have since converted the mansion and stables into luxury apartments. A block of new apartments has also been built on the site of the former squash court.

Mrs Dorothy Combe, widow of Charles Henry Christian Combe, lived at Cobham Court until her death in 1979. She was a well-known and much loved character who insisted on continuing to drive her small Austin motor car despite increasingly bad eyesight.

When Charles Harvey Christian Combe died in 1983 the Cobham Park estate passed to his son, Dominic, who now lives at Cobham Lodge and continues to oversee the management of the Cobham Park estate, which includes one of Surrey's few remaining dairy herds at Cobham Court Farm.

In recent years Dominic Combe has done much to restore the fortunes of the estate and the parkland is currently undergoing a full restoration, much of it being returned to species rich grass land and specimen trees. Whilst still remaining in private hands, the park provides a much needed lung of open space close to Cobham and a haven for wildlife. Buzzards can be seen hovering over the wooded parts of the estate and their distinctive call heard from afar. It is believed that otters are returning to the river Mole. The river footbridge at Ashford means that it is possible for the public to walk around the perimeter of the park and enjoy the views across to the old down or doune. Here there is a relatively unchanged and unspoilt landscape providing a sense of continuity with the past and a place of calm and beauty in an otherwise fast changing and overcrowded environment. Elsewhere on the estate, buildings are being restored and converted to provide accommodation – local people, where possible, being given a priority. A major programme of replanting is also being undertaken as dangerous and diseased trees are thinned. Old derelict railings are gradually being restored or replaced and buildings within the park such as the ice house and footbridges are being restored.

However, and in addition to the financial pressures of maintaining this historic landscape for future generations, there are now new pressures on the estate. The M25 motorway sliced through the estate in the 1970s and now it seems inevitable that a service station is to be built at Downside despite the fact that Cobham Park and most of Cobham south of the river Mole up to and including Bookham Common is likely to be recognised in the near future as an Area of Special Historic Landscape Value. At the time of writing there is still talk of a high-speed rail link passing through the area. Cobham Park with its long and chequered history has seen people come and go. Royalty, politicians, military leaders, writers and artists have all found refuge here. It is a timeless landscape that provides a stability and tranquillity much needed in these fast changing times. Long may it be so.

APPENDIX I

COMBE OF WILTSHIRE

Among the many thousands of precious records held by The National Archives at Kew (formerly the Public Record Office) is a charter dating from the early 13th century whereby John de Cumba granted to Thomas, son of Philip two crofts 'in my fee of Fitelton'.[1] It is from this Wiltshire land owner that the Combe family of Cobham believes it can trace descent.

Another 13th-century charter records the grant by 'Richard de Cumbe, son of John de Cumbe' to 'William, son of William, son of Osbert, one and a half virgates of land in Fitelthune with free pasture and pannage.'[2] This Richard de Cumbe married a lady called Sybil de Icklesham. An interesting story attaches itself to Sybil's grand-daughter. The grand-daughter, also named Sybil, was said to have been of masterful disposition. She frequently had differences with her husband, whom she outlived by 19 years, dying in 1247. Her determination of character is illustrated by her coming to the house of Philip de Burgeys in 1239 and having him arrested and carried off, bound, to Camberwell, 'where she kept him imprison for thirteen weeks, so that he lost the nails of his fingers and toes.' What event had led to this drastic action is not recorded but presumably Sybil believed that she had good enough reasons.

Richard de Cumbe was succeeded by his son Simon who in turn was succeeded by his son Richard who was appointed Sheriff of Wilts in 1289, a position which he held until shortly before his death in 1293. It was Sheriff Richard's sons who changed *de Cumbe* to *de Combe*. The son of Simon de Combe (1275-1300) was knighted and became Sir Richard

141 Seal of Sir Richard Combe, 1352.

142   Arms of the Combe family.

de Combe, Lord of Fitelton and Combe. From a document preserved in the British Library it appears that relations between the squire and the parson of Combe were not particularly cordial; for it is stated that Sir Richard de Combe, lord of Fytleton and Combe, presented the living to Sir Thomas Cok who served until 'the first pestilence' in 1348 (the Black Death). Shortly afterwards Sir Richard expelled Sir Thomas on account of some fault placed upon him by the latter. Sir Richard then appointed Sir Ralph de Douanton whom he also expelled for a whole year by reason of some scandal attributed to him by Sir Ralph, and then presented John de Aderne, whom he likewise expelled and recalled Sir Ralph, whom he expelled again after a year, and then presented Sir Roger Bacon, and agreed with him to remain and serve the chapel for all his life. Both the priest and Sir Richard died when the plague broke out again in 1361.

The Combe family continues to be heard of in that part of Wiltshire until the end of the 16th century. There is then a break in the link but it is surmised that John Combe of Compton, Amesbury, Todeworth and Combe was the father of John Combe of Shaston and Canne, living in 1503, from whom the present family can certainly claim direct ancestry without a break.

John Combe (died 1577) was Bailiff of the Manor of Barton by Shaston in 1545 and joint tenant with his father of lands in Canne, near Shaftesbury, called Formages and Barkers, with a 'Gryndstone myll' and the Mill-close. John Combe, son of John, was assessed at £10 'in goods' for the Subsidy of the Tithing of Tisbury in 1576. He was churchwarden of Tisbury in 1580 and in his Will, proved at Salisbury in 1600, he left bequests 'to my parische churche of Tisbury; to the Cathedral Churche of Sarum; to the church of ffountmell and unto the poor people there tenne shillings'. One of John Combe's grandsons was Matthew Combe, M.D. of Winchester (1662-1748), who is buried in the cathedral there.

APPENDIX II

THE 'FUNNY, FUNNY COMBES'

(From the Diaries of Susan Lushington of Pyports, Cobham)

1890

Friday December 26
(After attending morning service at St Andrew's parish church)

We talked with the Combes coming out – who asked me to come & skate this afternoon – so I went up … I had a nice funny time. I arrived and was told there was no other way through the snow except by Toboggan – so I found myself for the first time in my life going a terrific speed down the hill with no other guide than the little ? girl! However I arrived alright & Boyce Combe put on my skates for me. But I tried it in shoes & it wouldn't work at all which was very annoying & finally took them off – & tobogganed the rest of the time. The Combes have quite the funniest manners anyone ever had but I am sure they mean to be nice. Mr Combe was very nice to me & Boyce & Harvey were both nice. I had a little talk with Mr Deare too – who I like – also Ethel – they seem to be delightfully happy.[3] I came home with the Hewitts[4] but I don't much care for them. The next thing Wilfred appeared at 11 & Father & I & Aunt Alice walked him back to his home where he showed us his Oxford photographs. While we were there Florence, Boyce & Harvey came up & I had a long talk with Boyce & Harvey about Eton & Oxford. We came back to lunch & I hurried back to the Combes to skate – this time with my proper boots which were quite successful. Mr Combe put on my skates for me also Mr Deare who told me that Ethel had met Ludlow Coape-Smith [?] abroad! I think I got on with skating a great deal & I can very nearly do outside edge now. Mr & Mrs Dick Arnold who were there do it very well indeed.[5] The Combes gradually walked away in the funniest way & left us visitors still skating. I had a very good game of hockey first. Boyce & I against Wilfred & Harvey and they won. Unfortunately it had thawed for a little in the middle of the day & and so the toboggan wouldn't work. Came home to tea.

…

(The following extracts cover a short period during from the lead-up to Christmas through to the New Year 1892/3. Charles and Marianne Combe had gone to India and the young people left at Cobham Park spent much of this time with the Lushingtons. 'Leo' is Leopold Maxse, son of Admiral Maxse from Dunley, Effingham. Leo had married Kitty Lushington. He became a newspaper proprietor and she a London hostess. They were both used as models for various characters in several of the novels of Virginia Woolf who, as Virginia Stephen, had been a close childhood friend of Kitty. Another friend of the Maxses was the author George Meredith who lived at Boxhill.)

1892

Thursday December 22

… 'till in bounded the three Combes. It really was very funny to see Mrs Martineau carefully explaining to Evelyn that plumb-puddings ought to be made with Figs! While Lucy jumped up in the midst of talking to M & Florence and shouted to Mama – dates! I thought they would never go – but they did at last – & we had such fun with the Combes. Poor dears – they are simply revelling in being left alone – while Mr & Mrs Combe are in India – and *they* are so *happy* altogether. Ethel is there – & of course they feel they can do anything & everything – they stayed till I don't know when – & we made endless plans for entertainments, etc.

Friday December 23

We went first to Mrs Farr[6] who was really delightful. She invented a good many stories of Mrs Combe which, of course, I had to contradict!

Saturday December 24

We got to Ripley about 1 – but there was no sign of a meet. However at last I came upon the Onslows[7] – & we walked up the village together. The hounds did appear – but I don't think they did much hunting – it was much too hard. Then there were also the Combes, Harvey & Mr Deare & two friends riding – & the others all in the brake. I had rather fun talking to them – & asking for an explanation of Evelyn's most extraordinary note to me! Then there was Mr Bennet[8] – who I talked to & then Wilfred – but what has happened – he won't speak to me.

Xmas Morning

Off to church. I love Xmas morning service & the singing & everything was delightful – but oh the Sermon! It really was worse than I could have imagined! And when one thinks too how easy it would be to preach Xmas day – the whole world is before one – instead of which he went meandering on – for 25 minutes on doctrine!

Monday December 26

Suddenly in walked Florence & Ethel Combe! and were so amusing. We all sat and laughed over Mr Edwards visit this morning – & then they said the lake was in proper skating order & would I come. Of course I was overjoyed & started of the minute after lunch with Adele & the two children! Funny walking up to that house & not feeling *the* least afraid! We put on our skates on the island where there was a large fire – which was a joy. It was really too nice to see those children skimming along – they skate quite *capitally*. I found I was hardly at all out of practice & got on all right. I did a lot of outside edge with Harvey & talked to him about Stephen Latham who he knew at Gottingen! There was also another boy, a friend of his, who I skated with & altogether it was such fun. The Combes are really *dears* – they look after everyone so well & Florence lent Evelyn her skates – & put them on for her – & was quite charming. Then there was Janet Hollway – who of course I knew so much about & wanted very much to see, but when it came to the point I was terrified of her & couldn't say a word! They insisted on our going home by the garden way where I hadn't been for years.

Tuesday December 27
(At Cobham Station)

Then there were also the Combes – Florence & Gertrude seeing off a friend & they brought us back on their Irish car! It was so funny to go on one in England & we came like the wind. We had great fun. I sat with Gertrude – and Alice with Florence & I told them how alarmed I was at Miss Janet Hollway! They just put down at home & we then collected our skates & all went up there. Mildred[9] and Mary turned back after a time – Die[10] & I, Stephen & baby went on. Die can only just stand on her skates, scarcely that – so we had grand struggles to haul her along between us & poor dear once being wheeled along on a chair by Mr Rich she was upset and I'm afraid bruised herself rather badly – but she didn't feel it so much at the time – & went on any amount. Stephen can go along but not any figures or anything. Die & I stayed to lunch much to my intense surprise! It was too funny *being* in that house again. We went up to Florence's room to take off our things & she was so kind & nice. I sat between her and Mr Deare at lunch. Die was right at the other end. It is really pathetic how happy they are now that Mr & Mrs Combe are gone. It is turned into a Liberty Hall & everyone does exactly what they like. They took us into the drawing room the first instance after lunch to show us how they altered al the furniture! – & then there were simply *endless* photographs to examine. Then Die & I, Evelyn & Janet Hollway went up and spent I don't know how long with Ethel's baby. It is a perfect angel & Die was so happy with it. I think altogether she like going there – it amused her & no one could help liking the 4 girls themselves. I had quite a long talk with Miss Hollway – she is just going through the week before her brother goes to India for 5 years! I felt so sorry for her – Stephen & baby came up again after lunch and we all went back together for early tea before I went to the station to see Aunt Alice & Baby off by the 5 o'clock train.

Wednesday December 28

Stephen & I, Margaret & Mary all went up & the Combes were all too grieved to hear about Die & so nice about it ... we went back to the Combes again. Kitty & Mildred went up the house with Florence to see the baby & Margaret actually skated with Stephen & me & got on capitally! I enjoyed the rest and being just us 3 in the dark.

Friday December 30
(At Cobham Village Hall for a concert)

... the Combes arrived – 10 of them!

Saturday December 31
(At Cobham Park)

Charley Combe came forward and said howdedo – quite nicely – but fancy Percy & Harvey both being in smoking coats & trousers!! I think it was extremely bad manners ... & Harvey Combe so nice. Margaret, Mildred & my dear Die came up later. It was such joy to have her with one again – but of course she couldn't dance – only turn the organ & do piano duets with M! I did piano too for some time & then we all sang comic songs! It was really funny to see Stephen standing up to sing the chorus of The Man Who Broke The Bank At Monte Carlo! & even funnier still to see Mildred dancing lancers with Charley Coombe rushing round in the grand chain, shouting Tarara Boomdeay! It seemed firmly incongruous to be seeing the New Year in with the Combes of all people in the world! But there we were, I at the piano with Die at my side & all the others going round in a ring. We waited for the clock to strike & we came home directly afterwards.

1893

Sunday January 1

It snowed a little in the morning & Harvey Combe & Mr Deare were hard at work sweeping for which we threw them pennies in passing! Mildred and Mary insisted on helping of course & even Die said she was well enough to join too – but they all went home first. I went two or three long turns with Hollway – who I like so much. I was so terrified of her at first – but now I don't feel it a bit. She has a sort of abrupt way of putting things that one quite gets into after a bit. Leo went home to make the tea & we skated on – Margaret & Stephen, Kitty & Mildred & I alone, long after all the Combes had gone in – skimming about in the moonlight thinking of many things & times & New Years Days.

Monday January 2
(At Cobham Station)

… there were 6 Combes to see off Janet Hollway – so that after we had established them all in one carriage – there were 11 people to wish them Goodbye! … I came home in the brake with all the Combes & then after lunch Leo & I sped away to skate. The Miss Ravenscrofts appeared just as we were skating so I had to stop & see them a while – which after all I was rather glad to as Aunt Alice had told me such a lot about them. While we were all on the island a man's figure appeared on the hill. No one could guess who it could be – till Leo quietly remarked – if I don't mistake that is my father! In one minute all the Combes rushed at him – put on his skates – changed his coat – his hat & gloves (all of which he had brought a change of!) and then he was *shambling* along very unsteadily – but enjoying himself thoroughly. It really was too funny – he skated on for hours. After we all had to go up to tea! Leo at first said he took no tea – thinking to escape – I felt I had to take back his statement, unaparalled lie tho' it was! But it was really rather funny – when Kitty & Margaret arrived from Hatchford & Kitty overheard the Combes saying – can't we tempt you to take a little tea *for once*? Of course she said tea? – he always takes two cups at *least*! We go up then early & were shown endless photograph books & autographs etc. by Florence and then Leo discovered he had known Mr Deare when he was a tutor at Bournemouth – so retired on to the sofa with him for a very long time! Leo and I were the only two enterprising ones who sallied out to skate again after tea. The effort was terrific – but really it was lovely after a bit – the moon was glorious & threw a shadow the whole time which one went along – and for some reason or other one skated 10 times better than in daylight. Leo & I performed the most wonderful things & then had one turn around together, like a flash of lightening before going home. The evening was sad & lonely with them all & we came to bed early.

Tuesday January 3

I was to drive to Shere & I woke up & sprang eagerly to the window – but alas it was snowing fast. Kitty & Father drove to Leatherhead, Margaret stayed in bed. Leo & I sat & watched the weather. He wished it to continue – for if it cleared he had booked to go & see over the Combes electric light! I, of course, was longing & hoping it would clear but it never did & I had to be patient … M & I were just starting out for the Combes where we were going to dine – feeling very uneasy – when she (Kitty) suddenly appeared having walked from Effingham with a signalman through the snow! It really was a horrible anxious half hour as one didn't know where to telegraph or what to do. M & I found Ethel, Gertrude & Florence all in their dancing ? and they ? about a little afterwards but nothing very much. Of course we were a whole crowd & only 2 men – Captain Duff & Mr Deare who sat next to me. After Captain Duff danced the sword dance! – and then we began to play. I had no idea they would have enjoyed it anything like to much but at the end of everything they merely said 'Go on – something else –play that again while you are stopping to think!' I did any amount of Cavalleria & M did endless tunes – Mr Deare is really very musical & sat on the piano stool humming Hungarian tunes & bits from operas. The carriage we ordered at 10.30 was promptly sent round to the stables to put up till 12 & then we hardly got away – Oh how funny – but they are really so nice!

(It was on this occasion that Margaret Lushington recorded in her diary, 'Sue and I … dined with the Combes with fiddles; we played all night they adored it. Funny funny Combes.')

Wednesday January 4

… Then back to the Combes to skate – but goodness the cold. I don't think I have ever felt it more. I tried to skate but it was hopeless. I was numb up to my knees and nearly crying from the pain. Leo took me round once and then landed me at the end & I feebly tried to run home but I really felt quite ill & Margaret & Adele[11] rubbed me for a long time after I got in. Then arrived all the Combes to tea – Evelyn, Gertrude, Florence, Miss Adby & Miss Birdie Lamb! They said they must see us again & so invited themselves! It was very funny – but *very* nice! Olive came with them – & we had great fun trying on seven different fur caps onto Leo which the Admiral had sent him to chose from – he looked quite mad in all of them – but of course he chose the one he looked maddest in. However, in the end – we got him to decide on a sable one – which is quite aright. He was in tremendous form & would go on grilling Gertrude & Florence about woodpeckers and tennis courts etc! Olive drove him & Kit back with her to Dunley. The Combes stayed on – not quite sure whether I like Miss Lamb … The Combes themselves are dears & we bade a sad goodbye for of course when their father & mother are there it is all so different – it is quite likely we may not meet again for years!

NOTES

Chapter 1 – Early Days

1 Chertsey Abbey Cartularies, Surrey Record Society, no. XXXIV (1933) p. 318.
2 Calendar of Patent Rolls. Edward I. A.D. 1292-1301, p.183.
3 TNA Typescript itinerary of Edward I compiled in 1935 by E.W. Safford from the Close Rolls.
4 A full report of the excavation is to be published in the Surrey Archaeological Society Collections.
5 The probate inventory of Cobham Park made after the death of Harvey Combe in 1858 contains an intriguing reference to an item in the Library described as 'Roman Vase (found in 1833)'. The 'vase' has not survived. This raises the question of whether it had been found on the estate and, if so, was it actually a burial urn from a ploughed barrow predating the Roman period.
6 Now in Elmbridge Museum, Weybridge.
7 SMR 2006. Surrey Sites and Monuments Record. Surrey County Council: Kingston upon Thames.
8 For a full discussion on the use of the name dun in relationship to the landscape see Gelling, M. & Cole, A., *The Landscape of Place-names*, Shaun Tyas (2000).
9 Smith, R.A., *Romano-British Remains at Cobham* Surrey Archaeological Society Collections Vols. 21 & 22 (1908) and (1909).
10 Sheppard Frere, S., *The Excavation of a late Roman Bath-House at Chatley Farm, Cobham* Surrey Archaeological Society Collections Vol. 50 (1949).
11 The estate of Getinges became known as Yeatinge Fearme by 1598 and this is now Eaton Grange in Eaton Park – see Survey of the Manor of Cobham by Ralph Agas (1598) SHC 2610/29/3/1.
12 Landon, L., *The Cartae Antiquae Rolls. Pipe Roll Society* Vol. XVII (1939), no. 113.
13 Stenton, D.M., *English Society in the Early Middle Ages* Penguin (1951).

Chapter 2 – Citizen and Fishmonger of London

1 Chertsey Abbey Cartulary Vol. II, Pt. 1 Surrey Record Society (1958).
2 Royal Borough of Kingston KC2/2/6.
3 Manning & Bray, *The History and Antiquities of the County of Surrey Vol. 1* (1804).
4 Royal Borough of Kingston KC2/1/51.
5 This fraternity, or guild, existed in many towns and in earlier times it was known as the Shipmen's Gild: from the original guild is derived the Corporation of Trinity House which is still responsible for lighthouses and pilotage around our coasts. The existence of the guild in Kingston is evidence of the town's importance as a river port in those days and Bardsey, as a fishmonger, would have been keenly aware of the importance of the river to his business.
6 TNA E 134/30Eliz/Hil20 concerns an action in 1587 questioning whether an annuity of £6 13s.4d., issuing out of lands in Cobham called 'Pegotts and Dallaweyes', and other lands in Kingston 'lately belonging to Peter and Robert Bardsey', had been given by Robert Bardsey 'to find a priest in Kingston'. It has not been possible to identify the location of these lands in Cobham.
7 William Skerne was the nephew of Robert and Joanna Skerne whose magnificent brass can still be seen in All Saints church, Kingston. Joanna Skerne was the illegitimate daughter of Edward III and his mistress Alice Perrers.
8 TNA C1/26/447.
9 Malden, H.E. (ed.) *Victoria County History of Surrey* Volume Three (1911).
10 Surrey Taxation Returns – 15ths and Tenths 1332 Surrey Record Society (1932).
11 The Open Field system is believed to have been introduced by the Saxons. Communities such as Cobham would have a number of large open fields in which each villager had strips, usually called selions, scattered through the fields. At certain times of the year, after the crops had been harvested, the fields were thrown open for grazing. The system had many drawbacks. Time was wasted by farmers moving from one strip to another. Additionally, the multi-occupation of a field could lead to boundary disputes. In Cobham it seems that moves to enclose some of the strips and to combine them into smaller fields were already well underway by the 15th century. What remained of Cobham's open fields was finally

enclosed following an act of Parliament passed in 1779.

12 See Aston, G., 'Rural Settlement: the Toft and the Croft' in Astill & Grant, *The Countryside of Medieval England* Basil Blackwell (1998).

13 An archaeological survey and excavation, planned for the summer of 2006, has located the route of the old road and identified other apparent ancient features within a section of the park immediately to the south of the present mansion.

14 TNA E41/167 This deed of 29 June 1594 relates to land at Chilbrook Farm, Cobham and contains a covenant to produce earlier deeds. Amongst these is a deed of feoffment 6 Feb 17 Edward IV (1478) of land in Cobham from Roger and Margery Broke to Robert Bardsey and his heirs.

15 TNA C1/26/447, C1/34/32, C1/39/10.

16 TNA C1/282/19.

17 Abstract of Surrey Feet of Fines 1509-1558, Surrey Record Society 19 (1946) p. 15.

18 This grant, dated 14 February 13 Henry VIII (1498), is also listed in the schedule to TNA E41/167.

Chapter 3 – Royal Servants

1 TNA L.R. 2/190, ff. 264.

2 According to the antiquarian John Aubrey, a brass formerly in Walton parish church also commemorated John Carleton.

3 VCH Surrey Vol. III, p. 473.

4 P.C.C. 18 Porch Will of Dame Isabel Leigh of Stockwell. John Carleton was one of Dame Isabel's executors.

5 Richardson, W.C., *History of the Court of Augmentations 1536-1554*, Baton Rouge (1961).

6 Brayley, E.W., *A Topographical History of Surrey* G. Willis (London 1850) Vol. II, p.181.

7 Corpus Christi College to John Carleton 1 Oct 30 Henry VIII. This grant is listed in the schedule of deeds in TNA E41/167 (1594).

8 Walker, T.E.C., *The Chase of Hampton Court*, Surrey Archaeological Society Collections Vol. 62 (1965) and Thurley, S., *The Impact Of Royal Landholdings On The County of Surrey 1509-1649* in *Aspects of Archaeology & History In Surrey* Surrey Archaeological Society (2004).

9 The Act is reprinted in The Statutes of the Realm (1817), Vol. III, p. 721.

10 TNA LR2 190 – A Survey of the Manor of Cobham c.1547. Carleton also held by copyhold 'a toft and two virgates or virgin land once Gilbert at Grove's and a meadow called Blackwatermeade late William Tremayne's.'

11 Craib, T., *Surrey Chantries* Surrey Archaeological Society Collections Vol. 25 (1912)

12 Augm. Office, Misc. Books 233, fols 328, 328d.

13 Dascent, J.R., *Acts of the Privy Council*, II, pp. 190-2.

14 Information from *The Dictionary of National Biography* and from the Assistant Keeper of

the Muniments at Westminster Abbey. Gerard Carleton was also the Dean of Peterborough Cathedral from 1543-49.

15 Dudley Carleton had a brilliant career as a diplomat and courtier. He was an ambassador for 21 years and, while ambassador to The Hague from 1616 to 25, he used his diplomatic connections to secure works of art for English collectors. He negotiated with Rubens for an important group of paintings, including 'Daniel In The Lions' Den', which he gave to Charles I. In 1623 Dudley Carleton purchased Imber Court, Thames Ditton where he entertained Charles I and Queen Henrietta Maria in 1630.

16 In the 17th century this house was called 'the brick house' presumably because it was one of the first all-brick houses to be built in the village. It was later known as Leigh Hill House. In the 20th century it became known as the *Leigh Place Hotel*. It was demolished in the 1930s. The Cobham Church Warden accounts record Carleton as being rated for this property in 1629/30 and 1631/32.

17 DW/PA/7/10 ff.65r-v. On 29 June 1583 George Bicknoll of Kingston upon Thames 'taylor', son and heir of John Bicknoll late of the same 'wollendraper' deceased, son and heir of John Bicknoll late of Cobham deceased conveyed to John Gavell of Cobham a wood called 'Leache Rydon'. TNA E41/166.

18 COBPK/1/1/1(a)&(b).

19 TNA PROB/11/64.

20 SHC K145/6.

21 Matthews, L., *The Royal Apothecaries* (1967).

22 In 1595 Francis Gavell of Cobham leased to 'Edward Hemminwaie' of Croydon, the *Swan* inn and other lands at Street Cobham. Edward still held the Swan at the time of Agas's survey of 1598. The Cobham parish registers record the burial of 'Edward Hemingway an apothecary' on 1 October 1610. In August 1613 the Privy Council minutes record 'A warrant to Raymond Osbaston, one of the messenger's of His Majestie's Chamber, to make repayre to Cobham, and there to apprehend Thomas Hemingway, innholder.

23 Longleat House: Dudley Papers: DU/VOL.II.

24 TNA E41/106.

25 TNA E41/102. See also Bloxham, R.N., *On Some Minor Place-Names In Ockham And Wisley*, Surrey Archaeological Collection Vol. LX (1963) p. 60.

26 SHC K145/8.

27 The Cobham Church Wardens' accounts for 1629 record Walton being rated for 'woodland'. Other than this, nothing else is known about him.

28 SHC G45/1/9.

29 Walker, T.E.C., *Cobham: Manorial History*, Surrey Archaeological Collections Vol.58 (1961).

30 TNA PC2/52 p. 580 Minutes of Inner Star Chamber 26 June 1640 and HL/PO/JO/10/42 'Report to the

King re. Cause between Thomas Sutton & Simon Walter.

Chapter 4 – The King's Friend

1. This mortgage is recited in an Assignment of the Term dated 20 March 1749. COBPK/1/2/4.
2. Margaret was the daughter of Sir Humphrey Lynde, a theologian who was 'famous for his writing in defence of the Protestant Religion.'
3. Though it was unpaid, the post of gentleman of the privy chamber was nevertheless eagerly sought. The gentlemen of the privy chamber derived important and practical benefits from a post that involved them in no troublesome attendance. They were considered in law as menial servants of the Crown, which meant that they could not be compelled to serve in the militia or on a jury and that they were freed from parish and other offices. Further, and perhaps more significant, no household servant could be arrested for debt or on any civil charge without the leave of the lord chamberlain.
4. This was probably George Smithers of Downe Place.
5. B.M. Harl. MSS. No. 1422, f.8; no. 1470, f. 165b.
6. TNA LC3/25f.43. TNA Dartmouth mss oxD(w) 1778/6/132.
7. Surrey Quarter Sessions Records, Surrey County Council 1938, VIII, 160-1.
8. Carpenter is said to have been related to another William Carpenter who went to America in 1638 and from whom was descended Samuel Carpenter who settled in Philadelphia in 1683. Samuel was a member of the Provisional Council and Treasurer of Philadelphia from 1685 to 1711 and was named by William Penn, founder of Pennsylvania, as a trustee of his property in America.
9. TNA PROB4/12962.
10. DW/PC/7/1 Q.7.
11. Cobham Court later became part of the Cobham Park Estate when Charles Combe purchased it in 1905.

Chapter 5 – A Beautiful House

1. By profession this John Bridges was a solicitor and he and his family had served successive Lords Brooke for more than half a century. Perhaps Lord Brooke was godfather to Sir Brooke Bridges. The name Brook(e) was frequently used as a Christian name by successive generations of the Bridges family. See Hughes, A. (1987), *Politics, Society and Civil War in Warwickshire, 1620-1660* (CUP).
2. TNA PROB 11/659.
3. Middlesex Deeds Registry MLR 1717/6/11-12 and MLR 1746/1/168. 10 Soho Square is one of the only two surviving original houses in the Square.
4. TNA PROB 11/562.
5. John Bridges' account with Child's Bank shows him to have been speculating in the notorious South Sea Bubble. On 12 September 1717 he paid £5,584. for '4,100 India & 1,400 S.S. Bonds'. Unfortunately his later accounts have not survived and so it is not possible to tell whether he invested wisely.
6. The parish registers for Goodnestone record the burial of 'Mrs – Bridges, widow' on 13 December 1719. In the absence of any other possible related entry, this seems to refer to John's first wife Anne and perhaps the reference to her being a widow refers to her status when she and John married. Sir Brook's will had referred to Marriage Articles made between John and 'Mrs Anne Lewen'.
7. In 1717 £400 would have about the same purchase power as £42,000 today.
8. It is also possible that John was related to the Bridges family of Imber Court, Thames Ditton. Shem Bridges purchased Imber Court in 1672. He also owned the reputed manor of Heywood on Cobham's Fairmile and these properties were left to his nephew Henry when he died in 1711. After Henry's death the estates passed to his niece Anne Bridges, who married Arthur Onslow.
9. Ingamells, J., 1997, *A Dictionary of British and Irish Travellers in Italy 1701 – 1800* (Yale University Press).
10. Guildhall Library, MS 11,936/20, f.472.
11. Letter to the late T.E.C. Walker, F.S.A., now in the author's possession.
12. Jeremiah Freeland was the grandfather of John Freeland who later purchased and lived in 'Pyports', an old house opposite Cobham parish church, which he remodelled in the fashionable style of the 18th century.
13. I am grateful to Dr Steven Parissien for this information.
14. Rybczynski, W. 2002, *The Perfect House* (Scribner).
15. SHC G22/3/6.
16. SHC QS2/1/14.
17. I am grateful to Elizabeth Einberg of The Paul Mellon Centre for Studies in British Art for providing me with information about the Hogarth painting of Thomas Western junior, which is now in the National Gallery of Ireland, Dublin.
18. *The Travels Through England of Dr Richard Pococke, successively Bishop of Meath & Ossory, during 1750, 1757 & later years*. Edited by James Joel Cartwright, MA, FSA and printed by the Camden Society 1899.
19. COBPK/1/2/11(a)&(b).
20. The earliest known reference to 'Botells' is in 1318/19 when John de Bottele of Chertsey granted a messuage, land and rent in Cobham to Chertsey Abbey in exchange for other lands in Chertsey. In 1493 the Abbot of Chertsey granted to James Sutton 'one messuage and one virgate of land … called Botellys, lately Richard Hilton formerly Woodwardis'. Botells now appears to be the site of Cobham Lodge.

21 COBPK/1/6/9(a)&(b). These lands formed part of a messuage in Poulter's Lane, the old name for the Downside Road. The rest of the estate including the house was purchased by Lord Ligonier in 1758. Lancelot Barrett's ancestry can be traced back to Cicely Darnelly, a local benefactress and daughter of John Sutton, who owned land in this part of Cobham in the 16th century.

22 COBPK/1/2/5.23; COBPK/1/2/7.24; TNA PROB 11/883.

Chapter 6 – The Commander-in-Chief

1 A full account of the history of this house was published in *Country Life* on 15 November 1962.

2 British Library Add MSS 57318.

3 This is referred to in *Field Marshal Lord Ligonier* by Rex Whitworth (1958) OUP which is the definitive biography of Ligonier.

4 'Fragges' was an estate of dispersed lands lying close to Downe Field. In the 17th century 'Fragges' had been held by Edward Carleton, grandson of Sir John Carleton who had held 'Grovers' in the 16th century. Edward Carleton left his lease of 'Fragges' to his son Matthew. 'Fragges' later came into the hands of Sir Francis Vincent of Stoke D'Abernon whose daughter married into the Gavell family.

5 It is tempting to identify this property as one of those recorded in Ralph Agas's survey of the manor of Cobham (1598) being owned by John Sutton. Sutton's properties seem to have passed down through his daughter Cicely who married firstly William Crosley and then Richard Darnelly. After being entailed for at least two generations, the properties were eventually sold off in the 18th century.

6 COBPK/1/3/2(a)&(b).

7 The hanaper was the basket in which the King's great seal was kept.

8 The excavation report is awaiting publication in the Surrey Archaeological Society's Collections.

9 COBPK/1/8/1.

10 COBPK/1/5/3(a)&(b).

11 COBPK/1/8/20. 'Heathornes' (formerly 'Haw-thornes' or 'Haythornes') stood on the site of Cobham Park Laundry Cottage.

12 COBPK/1/8/24(a)&(b).

13 Ligonier was buried in St Andrew's church and, although there is a grand monument to him in Westminster Abbey, his resting place at Cobham was unmarked until a memorial plaque was placed in the war memorial chapel in 1973.

Chapter 7 – Scandal and Divorce

1 The *DNB* has an entry for Francis Ligonier.

2 William Fletcher lived in Church Street, Cobham, in the house now called 'Overbye'.

3 Trusler's unpublished memoirs are in Bath City Library.

4 19 Geo. III, cap. 15.

Chapter 8 – To Let

1 SHC: QS6/7/56.

2 There appears to have been some connection between Parry and Lord Rivers, father of Penelope Ligonier. In 1785 Mr and Mrs Thomas Parry of Cobham had reconveyed the manor of Cove, Hampshire to Lord Rivers following repayment of a loan of £1,500. Museum of English Rural Life: Wellington/A326/6.

3 John Courtney was an Irish MP and poet.

4 Robert Jephson (1736-1803), was an Irish dramatist and poet associated with Johnson, Burke and Garrick. Among his works is 'The Count of Narbonne', a stage version of *The Castle of Otranto*, the famous gothick novel written by his friend Horace Walpole.

5 *The Correspondence of James Boswell* edited by Charles N. Fifer (Heinemann, London). It is of interest to note that this letter was address as from 'Cobham Park', this being the earliest recorded use this title for the estate.

6 John Manners, Marquis of Granby (1721-1770), was famous for his military exploits and is now perhaps best remembered by the many public houses that carry his name.

7 For more on Raby see Crocker, G. (ed.), *Alexander Raby, Ironmaster*, Surrey Industrial History Group (2002).

8 Although the first part of the rambling and anecdotal *Memoirs of the Life of the Rev Dr John Trusler* was published in 1806, Trusler later regretted its publication and tried to suppress it by destroying all the copies he could find. The second unpublished part is now in the Bath City Library. Another copy, probably that prepared for the printer, is in the Lewis Walpole Library, Yale University.

9 Trusler was the uncle of Nancy Storace who became an established opera singer in the 18th century. She was the first 'Susannah' in Mozart's *Marriage of Figaro*. For more on Trusler at Cobham see Taylor, D.C., *Cobham Characters*, Appleton Publications (1999).

10 33 Geo. III, cap. 69.

11 Elm Farm on Cobham Tilt, which lies immediately across the river from Cobham Park, was purchased by Charles Combe in 1884.

Chapter 9 – 'One of the Most Unpopular Men in England'

1 *Town and Country Magazine*, 1771

2 Henry's sister, the Hon. Anne Horton, widow of Andrew Horton of Catton, Derbyshire, married the Duke of Cumberland, brother of George III in 1771. The king strongly disapproved of the marriage and it resulted in the Royal Marriages Act of 1772, which, still in force today, makes it illegal for

any member of the Royal Family to marry without the sovereign's consent. Another sister, Elizabeth, was notorious as a gambler and was imprisoned in the Fleet for her gambling debts. She paid a hairdresser £50 to marry her, which, according to the then state of the debtor's law, enabled her to procure a release. She went to Germany, where she is said to have been convicted of picking pockets and was sentenced and condemned to clean the streets chained to a wheelbarrow. The unfortunate woman poisoned herself.

3 *Town and Country Magazine*, 1771

4 The other 94 acres referred to in the 1805 lease were included in the sale to Harvey Christian Combe in 1806.

5 Cobham Lodge was bought back into the Cobham Park estate in 1905.

6 In his will Buckley bequeathed Cobham Lodge to Lady Caroline Treby Molesworth of Pencarrow, Cornwall and her youngest daughter, also named Caroline. Caroline the daughter was an enthusiastic meteorologist and after her death became more widely known through the publication of her *Cobham Journals* by the Meteorological Society.

7 In 1904 Charles Combe purchased Painshill Park and brought it into the Cobham Park estate.

Chapter 10 – The Lord Mayor

1 The *Waggon & Horses* was a public house that stood across the road from Cobham Park on the site now occupied partly by the Stud Farm and partly by Challenge Fencing.

2 CBPK/1/12/10.

3 Griffins Close and the farm house appear to have been between Downside Common and Downside Farm, south of the private road that leads from Cobham Park Road to Downside Mill. Gad also occupied 'Styles Ground' and 'Langleys' which were off Bookham Common Road, north of Chasemore Farm.

4 The Esher Place estate was eventually sold for £36,000 to John Spicer, a wealthy stockbroker. In 1843 John William Spicer of Esher Place became a partner in Combe's brewery.

5 An undated note in a file of miscellaneous genealogical notes made in the 1920s in the Hampshire Record Office states 'On 21st September 1787 there was sold a large Dwellinghouse in King's Head St., Andover with coach house, stables, gardens, orchard & meadow 5acres, late the property of Harvey Combe solicitor.' Ref: 38M85/BC/A10. For Harvey Combe's will see TNA Prob 11/1156.

6 Garlick, K. and MacIntyre, A. (eds.) *The Diary of Joseph Farringdon*, Yale University Press (1976).

7 In Alfred Barnard's *Noted Breweries of Great Britain & Ireland* (1889) this episode is attributed to a game of hazard played between Combe and Beau Brummel.

8 COBPK/54/1-18.

9 A watercolour of this property by John Hassell, dated 1822, is in the extra illustrated edition of Manning and Bray's *History of Surrey* in the British Library.

10 COBPK/1/19/2 & 10.

11 COBPK/1/19/8-9.

12 The estate accounts reveal the following statistics regarding the number of sheep kept by Combe and the annual income from the sale of their wool. 1806 – 156 sheep produced £40 5s., 1807 – 192 sheep produced £45 8s.8d., 1808 – 246 sheep produced £55 17s.4d., 1809 – 220 sheep produced £90.10s.

13 It is interesting to speculate whether this was one of the new drill ploughs invented by William Duckett who farmed land on Cobham's Fairmile.

14 Garlick, K. and MacIntyre, A. (eds.) *The Diary of Joseph Farringdon*, Yale University Press (1976).

15 Although the architect of the family mausoleum is not known, it is very much in the style of Sir Joan Soane, a leading architect of the day, who is best remembered for his work on the Bank of England which was tragically destroyed in the last century. However, a more likely attribution is that of J.B. Papworth, who was working at nearby Claremont at this time and who had earlier carried out improvements to Cobham Park.

16 Harvey Christian Combe in the *Dictionary of National Biography*.

Chapter 11 – Young Harvey

1 Thompson, F.M.L. (1963), *English Landed Society in the 19th Century*, Routledge and Kegan.

2 Two other members of the family later filled this post. Charles Combe was Sheriff in 1885 and his son Charles Harvey Combe in 1929.

3 Brayley's *History of Surrey*, 1st edition, 1848.

4 COBPK/45/1.

5 This is from a poem written by Theodore Hook while punting on the river at Thames Ditton.

6 Young, G.M. (1950), *Last Essays*, London, pp. 149 and 151.

7 COBPK/1/19/5&6.

8 COBPK/1/19/12.

9 COBPK/1/19/11.

10 Mingay, G.E., *A Social History of the English Countryside*.

11 For more on this incident see Taylor, David C. (1997), *Cobham Characters*, Appleton Publications.

12 COBPK/1/19/14.

13 COBPK/1/19/16 is a 'Book of Reference to the Map of the Estate of Harvey Combe, Esq.' made in 1855 and this contains a plan of 'New Garden, Conservatories etc.' as well as a plan of the newly laid out buildings and drainage at Down Farm.

14 S.W. Martins (2002), *The English Model Farm*, pp. 118-19.

15 Caird, J, (1852), *English Agriculture in 1850-51*, Longmans.

16 COBPK/5/17(a) & (b).

17 COBPK/3.

18 COBPK/9.

19 COBPK/11. The *Waggon & Horses* alehouse was owned by John Bourman in 1764. He had inherited it from his cousin John Covert in 1743.

20 COBPK/21.

21 COBPK/6&7 – There seems to have been a problem with the purchase of Chasemore Farm. Combe had purchased it on the basis that it was freehold. Shortly after completing the purchase he received a demand for rent from the lord of the manor. There then ensued lengthy correspondence between the lawyers acting for both parties. Combe wrote to his lawyer that 'Mr [Richard] Chasemore is quite as obstinate a person as his lawyer and is not to be influenced'.

22 COBPK/50-59.

23 COBPK/1/19/17.

24 The Cobham Vestry Minute Book for the period 1770-1891 is at the Surrey History Centre, Ref: 1865/3/1.

25 This canal led from the Thames at Chelsea Creek to Kensington, where there was a basin, near Warwick Road. It opened in 1828 but was many times beset by problems with silting and mud making navigation difficult, especially at low tide. The canal was eventually sold to the Bristol Birmingham and Thames Junction Railway in 1836. That company, now renamed the West London Railway, leased its line to the London and Birmingham Railway in 1846, leaving the West London Railway owning the canal.

26 Much of this and other information relating to the brewery comes from *The Red Barrel – A History of Watney Mann* by Hurford Janes (John Murray, 1963).

Chapter 12 – A New Squire and a New House

1 Charles Combe's daughter Gwendolyn later married Oswald Pearce Serocold, the son of the senior partner at Reid's brewery, thereby bringing family links into the business merger.

2 Estate and other papers refer to this as 'the old river', a description that raises questions. Does this mean that this was the original course of the river Mole? Is it conceivable that the large loop of the river round by Cobham Mill is an artificial construction? If it is artificial, when was it created and by whom?

3 COBPK/1/19/18.

4 The other is Wykehurst Place, near Bolney, West Sussex which he completed the year before Cobham Park.

5 COBPK/1/19/26.

6 This monument could not be traced in 2005.

7 ditto.

8 All the children survived into adulthood except Algernon who died in 1886. Margaret Lushington wrote to her sister Kitty, 'The poor Combes have lost their brother Algernon – 10 years old – of brain attack. Poor things it was so sudden it must be a great blow to them.' Uncatalogued letter at SHC.

9 Grant, J. (ed.), *Surrey: Historical, Biographical and Pictorial*.

10 Charles Combe to his son, 15 January 1884.

11 Uncatalogued letter at SHC.

12 Curtis, A. (2002), *Before Bloomsbury – The 1890s Diaries of Three Kensington Ladies*, 1890s Society.

13 *Cobham Parish Magazine*, June 1891.

14 This was probably Leigh Hill House, later Leigh Place, that stood on the site now occupied by the Leigh Place estate.

Chapter 13 – The Ending of the Old Order

1 This and other extracts from copy correspondence in a ledger referenced COBPK/1/17.

2 Anne died unmarried. Rosemary married William Clarke in 1944 and they had six children.

3 It is not clear whether this was the total staff list for Cobham or whether it included Bonchurch.

Appendix 2 – The 'Funny, Funny Combes'

1 Ancient Deeds C.2023.

2 Ancient Deeds C.2.2.227.

3 Mr Deare had married Ethel Combe.

4 The Hewitts lived at Ham Manor overlooking the river near Cobham Mill.

5 This was Richard Arnold, the son of Matthew Arnold who lived at Pains Hill Cottage, Cobham. Dick later became a close friend of Edward Elgar who under the initials 'R.P.A.' celebrated his personality musically in his Enigma Variations.

6 Mrs Anne Farr lived at what is now called Plough Corner Cottage, just across the road from Cobham Park.

7 Of Clandon Park and Ripley.

8 This was Thomas Bennett of Cobham Court, a keen huntsman.

9 Mildred Massingberd was a sister of Stephen who married Susan's sister Margaret.

10 Diana Massingberd, another sister of Stephen.

11 'Adele' was one of the Lushingtons' maids at Pyports.

BIBLIOGRAPHY

Airs, M. (1995) *The Tudor & Jacobean Country House: A Building History* Sutton Publishing Limited

Anon. (1770) *A Description of England and Wales*

Anon. (1770) *A New & Compleat History & Survey of the Cities of London and Westminster*

Anon. (1771) *The generous husband; or, the history of Lord Lelius and the fair Emilia. Containing likewise the genuine memoirs of Asmodei, the pretended Piedmontese Count* W. Wheeble, London

Anon. (*c.*1794) *New & Complete English Traveller*

Anon. (1820) *London & its Environs; or, the General Ambulator & Pocket Companion*

Anon. (1890) *The County of Surrey with Illustrated Biographies* St Albans, Truman Press, Victoria

Arnold, D. (1996) (ed.) *The Georgian Villa* Sutton Publishing

Arnold, D. (1998) (ed.) *The Georgian Country House: Architecture, Landscape and Society* Sutton Publishing

Barlow Gelderloos, D. (2003) *Eighteenth Century English Divorce: Laws and Social Practices and Their Impact on Gender Roles and Relationships. Pitt-Ligonier Case Study* Unpublished thesis

Barnard, A. (1889) *The Noted Breweries of Great Britain and Ireland* (3 vols) Sir Joseph Causton & Sons

Bird, J. & D.G. (ed.) (1987) *The Archaeology of Surrey to 1540* Surrey Archaeological Society

Blackstock, A.F. (2004) *Henry James Luttrell (1737-1821)* Oxford Dictionary of National Biography

Bladon, S. (1779) Trials *for Adultery or, the History of Divorces* London. Printed for S. Bladon

Blair, J. (1991) *Early Medieval Surrey – Landholding, Church & Settlement* Alan Sutton & Surrey Archaeological Society

Braybrook, N. (1959) *London Green: The Story of Kensington Gardens, Hyde Park, Green Park & St. James's Park* Victor Gollancz

Brayley, W.E. (1850 and later) *A History of Surrey*

Campbell, M. (1942) *The English Yeoman* Merlin

Cantor, L. (1987) *The Changing English Countryside 1400-1700* Routledge & Kegan Paul

Cartwright, J.J. (ed.) (1889) *The Travels Through England of Dr Richard Pococke* Camden Society New Series 44

Chalmers, J. (1985) *The English House* Methuen

Cherry, B. & Pevsner, N. (1983) *The Buildings of England: London 2 South* Penguin

Cliffe, J. (1999) *The World of the Country House in Seventeenth-Century England* Yale University Press

Collinson, P. (2004) *George Carleton (1529-1590)* Oxford Dictionary of National Biography

Colvin, H. (1995) *A Biographical Dictionary of British Architects 1600-1840* Yale University Press

Cook, O. & Kersting, A. (1974) *The English Country House* Thames & Hudson

Cotton, J., Crocker, G., & Graham, A. (2004) *Aspects of Archaeology & History in Surrey* Surrey Archaeological Society

Crocker, G. (ed.) (2002) *Alexander Raby, Ironmaster* Surrey Industrial History Group

Cruikshank, D. (1985) *A Guide to the Georgian Buildings of Britain & Ireland* Weidenfeld &Nicolson

Defoe, D. (1724 & 1742) *A Tour Through The Whole Island Of Great Britain*

Dyer, C. (2003) *Making a Living in the Middle Ages: The People of Britain 850-1520* Penguin

Falkner, J. (2004) *Edward Ligonier (1740?-1782)* Oxford Dictionary of National Biography

Garlick, K. & MacIntyr, A. (eds.) (1976) *The Diary of Joseph Farringdon* Yale University Press

Gelling, M. (1984) *Place-Names in the Landscape* Dent

Girouard, M. (1978) *Life In The English Country House: A Social and Architectural History* Yale University Press

Girouard, M. (1978) *The Victorian Country House* Yale University Press

Goldberg, P.J.P. (2004) *Medieval England: A Social History 1250-1550* Arnold

Grant, J. (undated) *Surrey: Historical, Biographical and Pictorial* The London & Provincial Publishing Company

Gutzke, D.W. (1984) *The Social Status of Landed Brewers in Britain since 1840* in Histoire sociale – Social History Vol. XVII, No. 33, University of Ottawa

Hadfield, M. (1969) *A History of British Gardening* John Murray

Harris, J. (1994) *The Palladian Revival: Lord Burlington, His Villa and Garden at Chiswick House* Royal Academy of Arts

Hobhouse, H. (1971) *Thomas Cubitt: Master Builder* Macmillan

Horn, P. (1980) *The Rural World 1780-1850* Hutchinson

Hoskins, W.G. (1955) *The Making Of The English Landscape* Hodder & Stoughton

Hussey, C. (1967) *English Gardens and Landscapes* Country Life

Ingamells, J. (1997) *A Dictionary of British and Irish Travellers in Italy 1701-1800* Yale University Press

Janes, H. (1963) *The Red Barrel* John Murray

Lees-Milne, J. (1986) *The Earls of Creation* Century Hutchinson Limited

Linden, J. (ed.) (2001) *Alfieri Revisited* Supplement to the Italianist No. 21

Major, E. (2004) *John Trusler (1735-1820)* Oxford Dictionary of National Biography

Malcolm, J. (1804-1814) *Modern Husbandry of Surrey*

Malinson, H. (2006) *Guildford via Cobham: the Origins and Impact of a Country*

Railway published by the author

Manning, O. & Bray, W. (1804-1814) *The History and Antiquities of the County of Surrey*

Martins, S.W. (2002) *The English Model Farm: Building the Agricultural Ideal, 1700-1914* Windgather Press

Martins, S.W. (2004) *Farmers, Landlords and Landscapes: Rural Britain, 1720 to 1870* Windgather Press

Mathias, P. (1959) *The Brewing Industry in England 1700-1830* CUP

Mills, D. (1980) *Lord and Peasant in Nineteenth Century Britain* Croom Helm

Mingay, G.E. (1963) *English Landed Society in the Eighteenth Century* Routledge

Mingay, G.E. (1963) *The Gentry: The Rise and Fall of a Ruling Class* Longman

Mingay, G.E. (1977) *Rural Life in Victorian England* William Heinemann Ltd

Mingay, G.E. (ed.) (1981) *The Victorian Countryside* Vol. 2 Routledge & Kegan Paul

Mingay, G.E. (1990) *A Social History of the English Countryside* Routledge

Nairn, I. & Pevsner, N. (1971) *The Buildings of England: Surrey* Penguin

Neeson, J.M. (1993) *Commoners: Common Right, Enclosure and Social Change in England (1700-1820)* Cambridge

Nichols, J. (1812) *Literary Anecdotes of the Eighteenth Century*

Orton, C. (ed.) (1995) *Celebrating our Past: Studies in local history and archaeology on the occasion of the 75th Anniversary of the Beddington, Carshalton and Wallington Archaeological Society* Occasional Paper No. 5

Parissien, S.P. (1989) 'The Careers of Roger and Robert Morris, Architects' Unpublished PhD Thesis Linacre College, Oxford

Picard, L. (2003) *Elizabeth's London* Phoenix

Postan, M.M. (1975) *The Mediaeval Economy and Society* Pelican

Rackham, O. (1987) *The History of the Countryside* J.M. Dent & Sons

Richmond, L. & Turton, A. (1990) *The Brewing Industry: A Guide to Historical Records* Manchester University Press

Rubenstein, W.D. (1981) *Men of Property* Croom Helm

Rubenstein, W.D. (1981) *New Men of Wealth and the Purchase of Land in 19th century Britain* Past & Present No.92

Rude, G. (1971) *Hanoverian London 1714-1808* Secker & Warburg

Rybczynski, W. (2003) *The Perfect House* Scribner

Schofield, P. (2003) *Peasant and Community in Medieval England 1200-1500* Palgrave Macmillan

Scott, Sir G. (1857) *Secular and Domestic Architecture*

Siseman, A. (2001) *Boswell's Presumptuous Task: Writing the Life of Dr Johnson* Penguin

Spring, D. (1971) 'English Landowners and Nineteenth Century Industrialism' in Ward & West (eds.) *Land and Industry*, David & Charles

Stenton, D.M. (1975) *English Society in the Early Middle Ages* Pelican

Stevens, I. (1996) *The Story of Esher* Michael Lancet

Stevenson, W. (1813) *Agriculture of Surrey*

Stone, L. (1984) *An Open Elite? : England 1540-1880* Clarendon

Taylor, D. (1997) *Cobham Characters* Appleton Publications

Taylor, D. (1999) *Cobham Houses and their Occupants* Appleton Publications

Taylor, D. (2003) *Cobham: A History* Phillimore

Taylor, D. (2005) 'The Combe family of Cobham Park Surrey: 1806-1920. Did it take "the third generation" to make "the gentleman", or could 19th-century brewers acquire gentry status without sacrificing their non-landed income?' Unpublished MA thesis for Roehampton University

Thirsk, J. (ed.) (2000) *Rural England* Oxford

Thirsk, J. (General Editor) (1967-2000) *The Agrarian History of England* 8 vols Cambridge U.P.

Thomson, F.M.L. (1963) *English Landed Society in the Nineteenth Century* Routledge & Kegan Paul

Thorne, R.G. (1986) *The History of Parliament: The House of Commons 1790-1820* Secker & Warburg

Victoria County History of Surrey

Vincent, E.R. (ed.) (1961) *Alfieri-Memoirs* Oxford

Walker, T.E.C. *Cobham: Manorial History* Surrey Archaeological Society Collections Vol. 58

Walpole, H. *The Letters of Horace Walpole*

Wark, R. (1972) *Meet The Ladies: Personalities in the Huntington Portraits* The Huntington Library, California

Watson, J.S. (1960) *The Oxford History of England: The Reign of George III 1760-1815* Oxford

Whitworth, R. (1958) *Field Marshal Lord Ligonier* Oxford

Williamson, T. (2003) *Shaping Medieval Landscapes* Windgather Press

Wilmot, S. (1990) *'The Business of Improvement': Agriculture and Scientific Agriculture in Britain c. 1700-c.1870* No. 24 Historical Geography Series

Wilson, R.G. (2004) 'Combe, Harvey Christian (1752-1818)' *Oxford Dictionary of National Biography*

Wood, S. (2004) 'John Ligonier (1680-1770)' *Oxford Dictionary of National Biography*

Wooldridge, S.E. & Hutchings, G.E. *London's Countryside* Methuen & Co. Ltd.

Wordis, J.R. (1982) *Estate Management in Eighteenth-Century England: The Building of the Leveson-Gower Fortune* Royal Historical Society

Worsley, G. (1995) *Classical Architecture in Britain: The Heroic Age* Yale University Press

Wrightson, K. (2002) *Earthly Necessities: Economic Lives in Early Modern Britain, 1470-1750* Penguin

The Surrey Record Society has published a number of volumes with material that relates to Cobham and the land that makes up the Cobham Park estate. The volumes concerning the Chertsey Cartulary, the Surrey Quarter Sessions; the Surrey Hearth Tax; the Surrey Eyre and Surrey Fines have been consulted for this book.

The chief sources of unpublished material used in this book are found in the privately held Cobham Park Archives (CobPk), the Surrey History Centre (SHC), The National Archives (TNA), the West Yorkshire Records Office in Leeds (WYAS) and the House of Lords Records Office (HoL).

INDEX

Entries in **bold** refer to illustration numbers

M. C. Combe Esqr   1890   Jany 7   1924

<table>
<tr><td colspan="3">

To W. HARDING Dr.
JOB AND LIVERY STABLES,
"WHITE LION" HOTEL YARD,
COBHAM, SURREY.

Fashionable Carriages for Wedding Parties. Livery Horses strictly attended to.
BROUGHAMS, LANDAUS & OPEN FLYS ALWAYS IN READINESS.

</td></tr>
</table>

1889		£	s	d
Oct. 16th	A Fly to the Laundry		3	6
28th	Do from " to Stoke st		3	6
Oct 31st	Bus from Stoke st, to Hotel, and to Cobham Park, & back to Hotel, and to Stoke st	1	10	0
31st	A Brake from Stoke st to Cobham Park	1	0	0
	£	2	17	0

Paid W. Harding
Jany 14. 1890

Mr C H Combe Esqr

To S. W. CHILDS,
THE "PLOUGH" INN,
DOWNSIDE, COBHAM.

WINES AND SPIRITS.

1923		£	s	d
Dec 27	To Hire of Rooms & Gas		15	0
9 Galls Mild & Bitter	1	13	0
6 Doz Minerals	1	1	0
28 oz Tobacco or Equivalent in Cigarettes	1	1	0
Waiters		9	0
To Washing 5 Table cloths		2	6
	£	5	1	6

Settled Jany 8th/1924
S. W. Childs
with very best thanks

Fol. 346.

Cobham.
Surrey.

C. H. Combe Esq
Cobham Park.

To
Messrs Hooley, Kitching & Gaskell.

To Professional Attendance

April 1919.   5. 0

£ -. 5. 0

Recd with thanks Dec 28 1920

With Compliments.

Telephones :
54 Cobham.
115 Leatherhead.
76 Ashstead.

COBHAM, Surrey,
and at LEATHERHEAD
and ASHSTEAD.

MOULDS, LIMITED
General Ironmongers and Complete House Furnishers.

UPHOLSTERERS,   CABINET MAKERS,   CHINA and GLASS MERCHANTS,
CYCLE AGENTS.   PLUMBERS, etc.   REPAIRS A SPECIALITY.

C.H. Combe Esq,

Cobham Park,

Cobham.   December 1919.

Date		Credits	Debits	
Dec 1.	100 Bonax cartridges.		17	0
2.	24 115 X 70 Osram electric lamps.		12	0
	6 toilet tumblers.		9	0
	To recaning folding chair.		12	6
8	1 wood mallett.		2	1
24	1 wood tap as 1/1 1/-		2	2
18	To making 2 gate hooks & staples.			
			6	0	3

2669
Jan 5 1920
COBHAM, SURREY
Received from C H Combe Esq Cobham
£ 6:
For MOULDS,